From FEAR to Faith

D1262824

MUSLIM AND CHRISTIAN WOMEN

From
FEAR
to
Faith

MUSLIM AND CHRISTIAN WOMEN

Compiled by
Mary Ann Cate
Karol Downey

William Carey Library
Pasadena, CA

Cover design and layout by Karen Brightbill

Published by   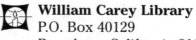 **William Carey Library**
P.O. Box 40129
Pasadena, California 91114
(626) 720-8210
inquiries@wclbooks.com
www.wclbooks.com

ISBN 0-87808-341-3

Printed in the United States of America

Table of Contents

Acknowledgments

By Karol Downey

It was with a mingling of fear and excitement that I first went overseas fifteen years ago to work among Muslim women. I had read many books on Islam, but few had anything specific to ministry among Muslim women. I basically had "on-the-job-training."

It has been exciting to see more material become available, much of which reflects the work of godly women missionaries who have gone before me in ministry to Muslim women. I deeply appreciate those who blazed a trail from fear to faith in missions.

MaryAnn's burden for touching the lives of Muslims for Jesus, as well as her vision for training missionary women, is a constant light to those of us who follow in her footsteps. She has often asked, "What kind of legacy is our generation leaving for the new generation?"

We hope that this book will serve as part of that legacy. It is dedicated to you, the reader. Our desire is to impart to you what experienced missionary women have learned through God's Word, their relationships, and their experiences in ministry to the Muslim world. We purpose to help missionary women minister more effectively, with better preparation and training, recognizing that all of us need to keep learning and sharpening our skills. We pray that this book is an encouragement to you, knowing that God is at work in the hearts of our Muslim friends.

Sue, Debi, Mary Ann and I were privileged to work together over several years in bringing much of this material together. I want to thank Beth Barron and Nancy Maurer for the many hours they put into editing this manuscript. Their help has been invaluable in putting this book together. Karen Brightbill, our graphic designer played a key role in producing the final format.

We serve a great God and acknowledge that all we are and have is because of him. May he be pleased to use each of us to bring his light to some of the least-reached peoples of the world—the women of Islam.

Preface

by Mary Ann Cate

On a sunny weekend in June, 324 women converged on the campus of Eastern College to attend the *Second Consultation on Ministry to Muslim Women*. Missionary, college and lay women interacted through worship and workshops around the theme, "That the Kingdom of God might come to the women of Islam." This book is the edited version of most of those sessions. We've arranged the contents to focus on concerns any woman working with Muslims might have: How can I be more prepared for this ministry? What are the needs of Muslim women and how can I address them? What are strategic steps to take in discipling Muslim background believers?

These have become critical questions as the world reawakens to the plight of women in Islam. College women are leaving behind lucrative career prospects to provide medical relief to women in purdah. Lay women meet North African immigrant women in the supermarkets and at aerobics classes and find that they do have much in common. Likewise, the roles of missionary women around the world, as language and cultural learners, friends and church planters are strategic in lifting the veils of darkness, hopelessness and fear that keep Muslim women from faith in Christ.

Believing that only women can reach beyond the heart veils of Muslim women, we who are mobilizers, care givers and trainers of missionary women are committed to equip and prepare the next generation of women for Muslim ministry. Read on, as women experienced in ministry to Muslims share their insights gained through years of witness among women behind the veil.

Introduction

May His Kingdom Come to the Women of Islam

by Sue Patt

A life devoted to the kingdom of God in ministry to Muslim women is not easy. So what do we do with our fears, needs and hurts when we are in the midst of our work? Where do we go in our minds and hearts when we are "honorably wounded" or bone weary? I can tell you where I go. I escape to the kingdom of God! That is, I readjust my perspective in light of what I know to be true about the kingdom of God. Come with me and see what I mean.

I first began to develop a practical understanding of God's kingdom when I took the Perspectives on the World Christian Movement course in the spring of 1980 while I was a student at Penn State University. Since then I have participated in more than a dozen Perspectives classes as a coordinator or a speaker. In Perspectives, the kingdom of God is defined simply as God's right to rule. Vine's Expository Dictionary defines it as "sovereignty, royal power, and dominion." Those of us who have lived in a country with a political monarchy might have a better understanding of this definition. When a king wishes something to be so, it is. He has the right to determine the affairs of state for his kingdom. His will is obeyed without question, contest or argument. Rebellion is not tolerated.

Think about what Jesus said in Matthew 9-10 as he was teaching the disciples to pray: "This, then, is how you should pray: 'Our Father in heaven hallowed be your name, your kingdom come, your will be done on earth as it is in heaven.'" God's will is not contested in heaven. It is obeyed completely and immediately. Jesus tells us to pray that God's will would be done on earth in the same way.

God has the sovereign right to rule on earth. But since God has given man free will, he will only exert his right to rule the heart which has voluntarily submitted to him. This biblical concept of submission is absolutely central to the kingdom of God. It is pivotal in the process of salvation, and it is essential to the redemptive purposes of the Father. Redeeming a people from all peoples for his name's sake is the age-old purpose of God. That is what God has been about since he chose the nation of Israel as one nation out of many within which to reveal His glory, and that is what God is about right now. We must watch and pray toward that end in the lives of Muslim women whom we love.

Oh, how I long for God's will to be completely uncontested in my life and in my heart! And I long to see God's will be completely uncontested in the lives of those around me. This is the spread of God's kingdom, and I am told by Jesus to pray toward that end. God's right to rule is to extend from the heart of the individual believer through the collection of believers called the Church. God equips the saints with various gifts for the fulfillment of His will as a corporate body (see I Cor 12).

Teaching about the kingdom of God is central to the message of Jesus. Jesus said, "Repent, for the kingdom of heaven is near" (Matt 4:17). He told many parables about the kingdom. It grows from something small, like a mustard seed (Matt. 13:31-32). Faith begins small, but it grows to be very strong. It is hidden like leaven, and it grows quietly, but pervasively (Matt 13:33). The kingdom of God is more precious than anything this world has to offer. It is like a treasure hidden in a field, or a very valuable pearl, which is worth exchanging all other possessions to obtain (Matt 13:44-46).

But the kingdom of God is a mystery, too. God did not merely establish a political kingdom with Jesus as the King. Jesus will return to reign as the undisputed, risen, conquering King of Glory. The mystery is that God's kingdom also exists now, in the hearts of believers, and in the future, as an eternal kingdom of peace. So why don't we see God's undisputed authority? Why are life and ministry hard?

This world is being ruled by the enemy of souls. "We know that we are children of God, and the whole world lies in the power of the evil one" (1 Jn. 5:19). Many people rebel against the authority of God and against his right to rule. There are two kingdoms, which are in total opposition to each other. This is the source of huge conflicts in our world. Conflicts, pain and suffering should not come as a surprise to us. In fact, if we put on "kingdom-of-God-lenses," then we recognize that the kingdom we gain through submission to God is much more valuable than the kingdom of this world. Even Jesus was no stranger to suffering! God's kingdom is stronger, but Satan's kingdom is at war with God's. We will see casualties around us; there will be casualties in our own lives. Knowing this should be a consolation to us: we need not be caught by surprise, and we can pray against the work of the evil one.

So, the present reality of the kingdom of God is that it is unseen; it exists in the hearts of believers who submit to God's right to rule; and it stands in total opposition to the kingdom of Satan who rules this world. What about the future kingdom? That's my favorite part!

Just as we know there is suffering now, we know that there is a day coming when suffering will come to an end. Revelation tells us that when God's redemptive purposes have been accomplished, there will be representatives from all the families of the earth who will stand before the throne to worship the Lamb.

> After this I looked and there before me was a great multitude that no one could count, from every nation, tribe, people and language, standing before the throne and in front of the Lamb. They were wearing white robes and were holding palm branches in their hands. And they cried out in a loud voice:
>
> > "Salvation belongs to our God, who sits on the throne, and to the Lamb."
>
> All the angels were standing around the throne and around the elders and the four living creatures. They fell down on their faces before the throne and worshiped God, saying:
>
> > "Amen! Praise and glory and wisdom and thanks and honor and power and strength be to our God for ever and ever. Amen!"
>
> Then one of the elders asked me, "These in white robes-who are they, and where did they come from?"
>
> I answered, "Sir, you know."
>
> And he said, "These are they who have come out of the great tribulation; they have washed their robes and made them white in the blood of the Lamb. Therefore,
>
> > "They are before the throne of God and serve him day and

night in his temple; and he who sits on the throne will spread his tent over them. Never again will they hunger; never again will they thirst. The sun will not beat upon them, nor any scorching heat. For the Lamb at the center of the throne will be their shepherd; he will lead them to springs of living water. And God will wipe away every tear from their eyes."

—Revelation 7:9-17

And there will be a new heaven and a new earth where there will be no more pain.

Then I saw a new heaven and a new earth, for the first heaven and the first earth had passed away, and there was no longer any sea. I saw the Holy City, the new Jerusalem, coming down out of heaven from God, prepared as a bride beautifully dressed for her husband. And I heard a loud voice from the throne saying, "Now the dwelling of God is with men, and he will live with them. They will be his people, and God himself will be with them and be their God. He will wipe every tear from their eyes. There will be no more death or mourning or crying or pain, for the old order of things has passed away."

He who was seated on the throne said, "I am making everything new!" Then he said, "Write this down, for these words are trustworthy and true."

He said to me: "It is done. I am the Alpha and the Omega, the Beginning and the End. To him who is thirsty I will give to drink without cost from the spring of the water of life."

—Revelation 21:1-6

All the tears we have shed in the struggle of this lifetime will be wiped away by the Holy One himself!

Often, while I am in worship, God gives me a glimpse of this scene: I am standing, usually in church, with my eyes closed and my hands raised, singing in worship. As God draws me into worship I become aware that I am not alone! I can see in my spirit that I am surrounded by a multitude of covered Muslim women who stand with hands raised, worshiping the Lamb of God. I have never experienced this without a flood of tears. The tears are a mixture of longing that it may be so, and of gratitude that I have seen it fulfilled. It's the kingdom of God!

It is the present reality in my heart, and it is the future reality as he receives the worship and glory which is due him.

May each one of us grow in our awareness of the kingdom of God: that we would see clearly his work in the hearts of Muslim women; that we would affirm the values of the kingdom of God when we see them lived out by our Muslim friends; and that we would be used by God to draw them deeper into his kingdom through the finished work of Jesus Christ.

Sue Patt has been on staff with the U.S. Center for World Mission since 1982. Sue has served in the Eastern Regional Office for the past 14 years in the ministry of recruiting and training field workers. She has co-led several short-term trips overseas and has been developing friendships with Muslim women for twenty years.

PART ONE
Missionary Women

Our Concept of God

by Dr. Jeanne Jensma

How many times have we heard someone say something such as, "I like to think of God as ..."? Maybe we'd like to think of God as being a certain way, but is that really who God is? We have ways of trying to make God into our own image, ascribing to him those qualities that we admire in ourselves. We think God is like us when we are at our best, instead of recognizing that God is who he has declared Himself to be.

Yet, what we think God is like impacts the way we talk to God, the way we talk about God, the way we interact with others, the way we think about ourselves, the way we perceive God to relate to us, and a host of other things. What we think God is like in our heart-of-hearts seeps out of our pores in a hundred ways. It is perhaps our ultimate witness, going far beyond our words.

At ALONGSIDE, we work with missionaries and pastors who have become wounded or burned out in the course of serving on the front lines of the Battle of the Ages. People come to us who have suffered great trauma. Others are exhausted, sometimes almost to the point of despair (cf. 2 Cor. 1:8) or have become injured in some way. In the course of our ministry, we have noticed the prevalence of a distorted image of God. No one arrives at our door saying that he needs some help regarding his concept of God, but as we work through the various life wounds that have accumulated, we discover together that the theology of the person's head and the theology of the person's heart sometimes do not match.

What do I mean when I use the phrase "God-image" or "God-concept"? Let me state first what I do not mean. I do not mean what you would write on a theology exam or in an application to a mission board. We know the right answers on paper. What I am talking about is the theology of our hearts, which governs how we respond to crises or stress. It is how we think about God in our hearts when our head knowledge is not sufficient for the pain of life in a fallen world.

The psalmist cries out in Psalm 77:8, "Has His unfailing love vanished forever?" Asaph knew God's love to be unfailing. But he was experiencing it as having vanished. The heart does not always experience what the head knows to be true. Tozer in *The Knowledge of the Holy* described this kind of knowledge as what a person "in his deep heart conceives God to be like." This, then, is what we will discuss today: our image of God, how it came to be, various distortions it may carry, and how to bring correction to those distortions.

Formation of God-image

We do not choose our God-image. It is in large measure bequeathed to us as children. Many of the key elements of our God-image are already in place by time we get to kindergarten. We often take many of those heart-beliefs about God with us into adult life and even to the grave. There are ways we can intentionally seek to bring about changes in our God-image, and sometimes the experiences of life modify or change our God-image. What we know of God when we enter kindergarten is not set in stone, but it is likely to form much of the backbone of our God-image throughout our lifetime.

My first memories of a consciousness of God took place in church. We did not have children's church. When we graduated from nursery at the age of two, we were taken into big people's church. I remember the church being somewhat dark. The stained glass windows were beautiful, but they didn't let in much light. I couldn't see the outside world. I sat near the back of the church. I suspect there was a reason for that!

I remember my mother whispering "Sshh." several times before the church service began. The organ music was beautiful, but quite somber. Eventually two doors on either side of the front of the church would open, and a number of men would file in. They all wore dark suits, white shirts, ties, and very serious looks on their faces. They sat down in unison, and as they hit the pew, the choir would pop up to sing the same song every week from Habakkuk to call us to worship: "The Lord is in His holy temple. Let all the earth keep silence, keep silence before him." (That was just in case I hadn't quite gotten the message from Mom's "sshhing" me! The whole choir was there to remind me to sit still and be quiet—two of God's most important rules.)

What impact did all that have on my God-concept? From a very young age I was deeply impressed that God-business is serious business. When we are consciously in the presence of God, we are to be filled with awe at his greatness and majesty. We are not to be casual with God, relating to him as a Divine Buddy. He is God and is utterly Other than what we are.

Great emphasis was placed on knowing and following God's rules. There seemed to be rules for everything. In church I had to sit still and be quiet. At home we had to pray before every meal, read the Bible, pray at the end of the meal, and pray again before going to bed. We were to fold our hands and close our eyes (and not peek) when we prayed. I was supposed to be seen and not heard. I couldn't do anything on Sunday except breathe, eat, go to church, read my Bible, and sleep. Once I came downstairs with wet hair. I was reprimanded for having washed it on Sunday. I must admit that I couldn't help thinking that God would rather have had me go to church with my hair clean than dirty! But somehow others did not see it that way. Rules were important. That's why the Bible story of the two men who tried to steady the Ark of the Covenant and were killed impressed me. It was clearly important to know the rules and know them well, because to guess wrong was to court death. So God to me was very much the Lawgiver and Judge.

I learned other attributes of God as well. Once the gas station across the street from my grandmother's house caught fire. The street was narrow, and grandma was afraid the fire would jump the street and destroy her home. She went from window to window, crying out to God to protect her home. I was too young to understand the danger. But I knew how important it was to fold hands and close eyes during prayer and it was very clear to me that grandma was praying. She was afraid of the fire, but I was afraid more of God striking her dead for ignoring the "prayer rules"!

God did mercifully spare Grandma's home (and grandma). Afterwards, I asked her why she hadn't folded her hands or closed her eyes while praying. I don't remember exactly how grandma answered, but she did make clear to me that God is the One on whom we call when we are in danger, and he is our Protector. With the full blaze of the gas station fire etched so vividly in the background, Grandma's words about God being our Protector went deep into my young heart.

It is these early childhood relationships and experiences—or sometimes the relationships and experiences we encounter with our spiritual mentors, if we come to Christ after childhood—that greatly impact our sense of what God is like. From my background, I learned that God is a God of majesty; God is a Lawgiver and Judge; and God is a Protector. These are the core concepts of my God-image. We are bequeathed such concepts by the words we hear, but even more by the nonverbal messages that we perceive in the "God-people" in our lives. We take a little bit of Mom, a bit of Dad, a bit of Grandma, something of various Sunday school and Christian school teachers, and a big piece of the nice lady up the street who has the neighborhood kids over for milk and cookies and a Bible story. Especially if there are commonalities among these people, we unconsciously assume that God is like that, too.

In many ways, I had a spiritually rich heritage, but not without drawbacks. In third grade, during daily vacation Bible school we were working on a craft project. On the side of it were the words, "God is love." I remember the sense of wonder that filled me as I blurted out the words, "Oh, what a nice idea! I wonder who thought of it!" Clearly the concept that God was a God of love had not become part of my core heart beliefs about God. How could I have missed that?

I come from a very Dutch background. The Dutch people have some wonderful traits. They are hard-working, logical, disciplined, organized, and faithful. But their strong emphasis on these traits may cause them to seem cold and distant compared with many other ethnic groups. I grew up surrounded by God-people who were relatively cold and distant. It was natural to assume on an unconscious level that since most of the God-people I knew were cold and distant, God must be like that, too. I knew the song, "Jesus Loves Me," but that's not the song that went through my head regularly as a little kid. The song that went through my head was this one: "You cannot hide from God. His eye is fixed on you. Wherever you go, whatever you do, you cannot hide from God." God was the Sovereign, Omnipresent Law-giver and Judge—but cold and distant. The ethnicity and personality style with which I was raised had tremendous impact upon this area of imbalance in the God-concept that I was bequeathed even before kindergarten. To this day there is an element of that imbalance, although it has been modified by subsequent people and experiences that God has brought into my life and by intentional effort on my part to examine and bring correction to various distortions in my God-image.

Cultural factors can also have an impact. How might Islamic culture influence the God-image that your children develop? How might it impact you as you live within its context? What others say about God impacts our God-image, but what they live out in terms of their deep heart-concept of God impacts us even more deeply.

Likewise, what we teach others about God with our words has influence. But what we teach with our lives and our relational style out of our deepest heart has much greater influence. We need to examine our hearts to make sure that our heart-concept of God and the nonverbal teaching that spills out through our lives gives an accurate testimony to who God is.

Distortions of God-image

The God of Impossible Expectations

Many missionaries and other servants of God have a God of Impossible Expectations, particularly people who are first-born in their families. A lot is expected of the first-born. Parents can't wait for the first word, the first step, the first "this" and the first "that." These firsts often are very important to parents, almost as though their reputation as parents is at stake in the outcome.

It is easy for first-borns to feel that, no matter how much or how well they do, it is not quite good enough! Parental eagerness often leaves first-borns with the sense that something more is always expected, that they have to rise to ever higher levels of performance to please their parents. Is it any wonder that they feel God expects ever higher levels of performance from them, as well?

And even some who are not first-borns have a great deal expected from them: "Why only a 'B+' in history when you got an 'A' in everything else?" "You made second chair in the trumpet section—too bad that you didn't make first when you were so close." Many of these messages are never spoken, yet they are clearly communicated expectations. Whatever is important in the family tradition—sports, academics, music, or church involvement—is an area in which a child can feel great pressure to perform in order to fulfil unrealistic expectations. Teachers can add to this sense of impossible expectations, too: "Ted is not living up to his potential." What a heavy burden it can be to have great potential in parents' or teachers' eyes!

If a child grows up with a continual sense of pressure to move toward the next developmental milestone or the next expected achievement, why would he not also sense that God always expects more from him? And thus the child, and later the adult, in his deep heart conceives God to be a God of unrealistic and increasing expectations. No matter how much one may preach a God of grace, if a missionary is a workaholic or a perfectionist in ministry, his life teaches that God is a God of Impossible Expectations. What our lives teach goes far deeper than what our mouths teach.

The Bookkeeper God

The Bookkeeper God keeps track of all the things I do that are right and all the things I do that are wrong. Whichever side weighs the heavier determines whether I am in his favor or in his disfavor. It's not a salvation thing—that has been secured. But it's a matter of relationship on a daily basis. When God does not provide the funds to buy the property that the church needs, then I say in my heart of hearts that I probably did not pray enough or believe enough or do-something-else enough. On God's balance sheet, I am found wanting, and so God is withholding blessing from me and my ministry.

This kind of "Bookkeeper God" begins in early childhood with parents who shower affection on their children when they like the children's behavior but withhold their affection when they dislike the children's behavior, instead of providing firm—but still very loving—discipline. The child grows into adolescence strongly suspecting that the team lost the basketball game because he had failed to have his quiet time that morning and God was teaching him a lesson. God is keeping an account of all good and bad behavior; the absence or presence of blessing in everyday life is a result of the current balance in one's account. Sometimes the desire to have a positive balance can even be one of the driving forces propelling a person into ministry.

The Impersonal, Distant God

There is also the Impersonal, Distant God. I know him well! I grew up with this God. He is a truly awesome God who is way out there, way up there and all-powerful, but not very approachable. Intimacy with this kind of a God is almost impossible. I worship him, I obey him, but sometimes it's hard to love him in my heart-of-hearts, because I certainly don't feel his love for me.

Children inherit this kind of God-image from cold, distant parents and other relatives. Such children grow up in a culture in which there is quite a bit of emotional distance between people, including between children and parents and between the parents themselves. If the God-people we are exposed to growing up relate to us in a distant way, we are likely to unwittingly develop the concept deep in our hearts that God also holds us at a distance, that we cannot know him very well or experience much closeness to him or intimacy with him.

The God Who Winks at Sin

Coming from my background, there wasn't much chance of developing this particular distortion. However, some people come from very permissive backgrounds with few absolutes and little discipline. They are in danger of developing a concept of God as a kindly, old gentleman who is very understanding and forgiving to the point of letting his children get away with just about anything. Love predominates, and holiness recedes among God's attributes. Perhaps God is even a bit mischievous, secretly delighting in "cute" misbehavior. This may reflect an earthly father who takes joy in the rascally adventures of his children, reminiscent of some of dad's earlier years and wilder days. This God is soft on sin and long on patience and tolerance. There is much in Western cultural values to bequeath this image of God to children growing up in this culture.

The God Who Abandons

Some children grow up with parents or other caretakers who are not available when needed. They promise to come to the ball game or concert, but something comes up and the parents fail to show up. The child is sick and stays home from school and the parent makes sure juice and videos are available but then goes to work, leaving the child alone. Or a child is warned in the store, "If you don't stop whining and asking for that toy, I'm going to leave you here and not come back for you until tomorrow." Even though the parent does not follow through, the threat creates a sense of abandonment. In other cases, Dad may be a tribal evangelist, out in the bush more than he is home, missing many important events in the child's life. If a child feels his primary caretakers have left him in the lurch fairly often, he is likely to doubt that God is "there for him" as well and will have difficulty developing a deep trust in God.

The God of Shattered Dreams

This God-image is one I see fairly often in my office. A Christian worker has a dream of doing some wonderful things for God, and believes that the dream is from God. But something happens and the dream becomes shattered. The worker labors for four years evangelizing an area and establishing a small church. After a short furlough, there is no sign of any believers or any church. Nine years is invested in translating the Scriptures into the mother tongue of a certain people group. When the translation is almost done, there is a fire and all of the work goes up in smoke—literally. Did God not want these people to have his Word in their language? Of course he did! Could God not have stopped the fire? Of course he could! Then how does one understand what happened? Was the ministry not from God? Next time such a missionary dreams of serving God, there will be insecurity regarding whether the dream is from God or not.

How does one relate to the God of Shattered Dreams? Most of us can survive one dream being shattered, but what about two? Or three? We cannot be dishonest with God, so what do we say to him? Like Jacob of old, we have to wrestle with this God of Shattered Dreams, being honest with him about our grief, anger, and confusion. We must learn how to grab onto him saying, "I will not let You go until You bless me."

The Abusive God

I don't like this term, but this is how some people think of God. They have been so deeply hurt so early in life by the people who are supposed to love them that they think God is like that as well. I think of the missionary who sat in my office and told me about being roasted in the oven by his mother when he was only three years old. The burn marks on his body were a constant reminder. A mother who would burn her child in the oven is a mother who does many other horrible things, and does them often. This missionary said, "I don't trust God. I know he exists. I know he is all-powerful. I know I have to obey him. He gave the Great Commission, so I know what I have to do to obey him. But I don't trust him. What kind of a God would give a little boy a mother who would roast him in the oven?"

Whatever theological answers we might give to that on an exam in a theology class, in the school of life, with the burn marks still visible and with the man looking you right in the eye, there is not a lot that can be said. The man needs empathy at that moment. Maybe theology would be helpful at another moment, but at that moment the man mostly needs compassion and understanding and someone who knows how to "weep with them that weep," including with grown men whose little-boy hearts are still raw with pain from yesteryear. People who have often been deeply abused as children may think of God as abusive, because he is all-powerful but did not stop the abuse of their childhood.

The Sexist God

Some people grow up in a culture in which women are considered to be property. They are abused and not adequately protected by the law in lands where only men have rights. How could a girl grow up in such a culture without thinking of God as sexist? Culture can greatly influence one's concept of God. Rearing daughters in Islamic culture exposes them to the possibility of adopting some very low views of women; this can deeply impact their understanding of who God is and how he sees them and relates to them.

Other common distortions, particularly Islamic

In an article I recently read about what brings Muslims to Christ, one Indonesian Muslim is quoted as saying, "God is universal and has no family. There was no way of knowing what God was like." What brought this man to Christ was the unconditional love that characterizes the Christian God. The man recognized this principally by the way believers treated one another, manifesting the unconditional love that the Holy Spirit placed in their hearts! Furthermore, concepts of God as Friend and as Father were instrumental in his coming to Christ. These were very attractive images of God in comparison to the impersonal God of Islam.

I am not well versed in the particular distorted concepts of God that are part of Islamic beliefs and culture. But it is important for those who minister in this context to understand that these distortions will impact how your listeners unconsciously twist your words to fit concepts of God that they already hold. These distorted concepts of God may also affect the image of God that your children are bequeathed if they are reared in this culture. Examine these issues carefully and talk about them in your families. You can make a difference not only by the words you use in consciously teaching but also by your life and relational style.

Correcting of Distortions of God-image

Discern the distortion

We cannot correct something until we know what is wrong. For example, if we step outside and the breeze messes up our hair, we cannot put it back in place until we look into a mirror and see the problem! Similarly, until we know what is out-of-proportion in our concept of God, we cannot bring correction to it. We first need to discover what may be problematic in our perception of who God is.

How do we do that? One way is to ask someone who knows us well—perhaps someone who prays with us often, someone who has an intimate knowledge of our walk with the Lord. We ask such people if they have come to see any imbalance in our understanding of God's person.

Another approach is to think logically. Given our background in terms of family dynamics, cultural/ethnic considerations, specific events in our life or the life of our family, what would we logically suspect could be the distortions that might occur in our God-image?

Certainly it is important to ask God to show us what distortions of him we unwittingly entertain. He is zealous for being known, and he is able to guide and challenge us, whether directly or through resources that he brings into our life. God has a vested interest in having his servants know and represent him accurately. Part of the Holy Spirit's job is to lead us into truth: he can help us understand where our concept of God is warped or imbalanced: and he can lead us into having heart-truth as well as head-truth regarding who God is.

Discover and affirm the truth

The second aspect of correcting distortions in one's God-image is to discover or re-discover and affirm the truth about God. Scripture is marvelously balanced. That's why several theological arguments have been able to flourish for centuries among equally committed believers in the Lord Jesus Christ! Scripture teaches that God is absolutely sovereign. Scripture also teaches that human beings can make genuine choices for which they are responsible. This is not a contradiction, but rather a paradox—two aspects of truth that we have difficulty fitting together. Giving each aspect its due attention in a balanced way is a challenge. And thus it is also with the various distortions of God-concept. Often it is not that there is no truth in the distortion, it's that the distortion is imbalanced. What we need is for the Holy Spirit to work within us to bring the various attributes of God into balance in our understanding of him.

Take, for example, the God of Impossible Expectations. It is not a good idea for a person who largely experiences God in this way to meditate a lot on the verse, "Be perfect therefore, as your heavenly Father is perfect" (Matt 5:48). That's a great verse for the wayward or the sluggard but not for the perfectionist who has a God of Impossible Expectations! That person needs to memorize and meditate more on passages such as, "For he knows how we are formed, he remembers that we are dust" (Ps. 103:14). Such people need reminders that God knows our limitations and does not expect more of us than we can be or do.

Or take the Impersonal, Distant God. The person who experiences God to be distant and impersonal does not need to spend a lot of time contemplating the passage that talks about God's throne being in the heavens and the earth being his footstool! A passage that would be more helpful for that person to memorize might be verses such as Jeremiah 31:3: "I have loved you with an everlasting love; I have drawn you with loving-kindness." Or, "The Lord is near to all who call upon Him, to all who call upon Him in truth" (Ps 145:18).

For the Bookkeeper God there are verses such as "All our righteous acts are like filthy rags" (Is 64:6). Or the teaching that if we have broken the law in even one point, we have broken the whole law (Jas 2:10). Or the fact that Christ has kept the law in our stead and died and arose again to pay our debt in full and that God sees his children as already righteous in Christ (Rom 10:4). God's bookkeeping is very different from ours!

What about the God Who Winks at Sin? What of the passages such as the verse that God is too holy to even look at sin (Hab1:13)? And the God Who Abandons—Jesus promised, "I will never leave you nor forsake you" (Heb 13:5). And the God of Shattered Dreams—from Jeremiah (29:11) come the words, "I know the plans that I have for you, says the Lord, plans for good and not for evil, to give you a future and a hope." As for the Sexist God, Galatians 3:28 teaches that God does not view men as the superior and privileged gender but that God views everyone as having equal value in Christ.

For all these distortions in what we in our deep hearts conceive God to be like—all these unconscious attributions bequeathed us by our family and culture—there is correction available in God's Word. "All Scripture is inspired by God and is profitable for doctrine, for reproof, for correction." (2 Tim 3:16). Choosing the passage that provides the corrective balance, memorizing it, and meditating on it often will go a long way to bring the correction that is needed. And the Holy Spirit is faithful to bring such passages to our minds and work them "through and through" in our hearts as we work together with him to bring maturity (including balance in our God-concept) to our Christian walk (Phil 2:12).

Target relational learning

Relational learning is the third aspect in bringing correction to our distortions about who God is. Such learning goes deeper into our core than learning from words alone. Just as the relational style of those around me as a child taught me that God is cold and distant, so it was the relational style of those around me in my early adulthood that taught me that God is love.

When I first arrived in Brazil as a missionary, I soon realized that life was going to be quite different from that of my Dutch Reformed background! Upon entering church, everyone greeted me with a hug and several kisses on the cheek. Before leaving church, this was repeated. And it happened every time we went to church. I think I had more hugs and kisses that first week in Brazil than I'd had in my whole life to date.

It didn't stop there. One missionary family invited me to dinner every Thursday night. Upon entering their home, each of the children in turn gave me a hug, then Mom, then Dad, and again upon leaving. I was pretty uncomfortable with all this affection. But I realized that if I were going to be a good missionary in Brazil, I would have to develop a degree of comfort with and appreciation for all the affection and warmth that is so freely shared. It took me nearly a year to grow accustomed to the physical expressions of emotional warmth. It took two years before I felt able to naturally extend it to others. In the meantime, I became closer with this one family than I had ever been to anyone else, with generous affection paving the way. And one day I realized that I felt much closer to God than I had ever felt. I was able to experience his love which before had been merely a theological concept. But now I was actually able to feel and experience God's emotional warmth!

While I fully believe that God can miraculously make himself known as a loving God regardless of our backgrounds, I also believe that God normally operates upon the principle of 1 John 4:20: We cannot love God, whom we have not seen, when we don't even love our brother, whom we have seen. This is a principle that God created within the human personality. What we experience with people, we can then experience with God. He often uses the people around us to carve out a "love place" within us, and then he fills it.

This is why relational learning is so important. I did not choose relational learning. God chose it for me. But we also can choose it for ourselves. Look for someone whose God-image is more balanced than yours. Make friends with that person. Pray often with that person. Let that person impact you in ways that the Holy Spirit can use to bring balance deep within you—in your heart and not just in your head.

What we think about God, "what we in our deep heart conceive God to be like," to use Tozer's words, is a tremendously important part of our witness. It comes out in ways of which we may not be aware. It impacts people far more deeply than even the words we say or teach. Our relational style will teach more about our God-concept in deeper ways than our Sunday school lessons, sermons or Bible studies. We need to take heed to ourselves in order to care well for those to whom God has given us the privilege to minister (Acts 20:28). We need to examine our own God-image, discern the distortions and correct them through intentional application of God's Word and through relational learning.

Dr. Jeanne Jensma has been the Director of Counseling for four years at ALONG-SIDE, a ministry of restoration and refreshment for missionaries. Jeanne has a pas-

sion for promoting growth and wholeness in Christ in missionaries in order to help maximize the effectiveness of their ministries. Jeanne spent over a decade in Brazil as a missionary before serving at ALONGSIDE.

Facing Fear

by Dr. Jeanne Jensma

The Purpose of Fear

We are emotional beings because we are made in God's image and God is a God of deep passions. The best-known verse in Scripture, John 3:16, tells us that God so loved the world. The Old Testament also talks of God's love: "I have loved you with an everlasting love" (Jeremiah 33:3). God's anger is spoken of in many places in the Old Testament and even the New Testament, which says that God pours out his wrath against ungodliness (Romans 1:18). God also grieves. From the Old Testament we learn that God grieved because he had made man. According to Scripture God feels joy. Zephaniah 3:17 tells us that God rejoices over his people with singing. Did you know that we have a singing God? And we learn in the gospels that there is great joy in heaven when even one sinner repents.

Then there is the Lord Jesus: how he loved! One of his disciples felt that love so keenly that he always referred to himself as "the disciple whom Jesus loved." Jesus felt grief, weeping over the death of Lazarus even though he knew he would raise Lazarus from the dead in three days. We know from the story of the moneychangers in the temple that Jesus could get very angry. In fact, he regularly called the Pharisees names like "brood of vipers" and "white-washed tombs." He experienced loneliness, wanting the support of his best friends in the Garden of Gethsemane. And he experienced fear, calling out to his Father, "If there be any other way, please take this cup from Me." The Lord Jesus experienced all the emotions that are common to human beings, and he demonstrated these deep emotions throughout his life.

We also are emotional beings because we were created in God's image. Most of us are okay with emotions like love, joy, peace, and compassion. But what of the negative emotions? What part do they play in our lives?

God gave us the so-called "negative emotions" to help us deal with a fallen planet. We would have had no use for them in Eden. Anger gives us the energy to deal with injustice, to right something that is wrong. In Eden, there was no injustice, and so anger was not needed. Grief helps us to heal after experiencing great loss. In Eden, there were no losses, and therefore we had no need to grieve. Guilt signals us that we have done something wrong, and motivates us to acknowledge and forsake sin, making restitution if possible. And fear—the subject at hand—also serves a purpose. Fear alerts us that danger is present. Fear empowers us to run from danger or to fight danger. Although fear was not needed in Eden because there was no danger (until Satan entered the picture), it is a God-given emotion that equips us to live in a fallen world that has many dangers.

Sometimes you hear it said in conservative Christian circles that fear is wrong, that it is sin; but make no mistake, fear is God-given to equip us to deal with very real danger in this world. Even the Apostle Paul stated in 1 Corinthians 2:3 that he had been afraid: "I came to you in weakness and fear, with much trembling." Being afraid is not wrong, but rather how we handle fear can be key in determining if we are rightly or wrongly afraid.

Kinds of Fear

Anticipatory fear

Sometimes we fear before a danger is actually present. We use the word "dread" for this kind of fear. It is going to happen, and we cringe at the thought. It might be a difficult conversation we expect to have with another person. It might be surgery for which we are scheduled. It might be a potentially dangerous mission that we are about to undertake. A good aspect of this fear is that it often motivates us to rehearse in our minds what we will do if the other person says "this," or what arrangements to make in case we cannot fully care for ourselves after the surgery. This is a proactive response to dread, which motivates us to carefully do our homework ahead of time. We can make responsible plans for "the worst," while hoping for "the best."

The difficulty with this kind of fear comes when we continue to dwell on it even after we have done all that we can to prepare to meet the danger. When our minds are filled with dread instead of being filled with the good kinds of thoughts described in Philippians 4:8, fear no longer serves the purpose for which God intended it. Fear becomes sinful when we choose to allow dread to take over our minds, rather than using it to equip us to deal with the dangers of a fallen world.

Retrospective fear

This is a past danger that we keep replaying in our minds. Each time we replay it, we again experience feelings of fear, perhaps even terror. Retrospective fear can be beneficial. It enables us to evaluate whether there might be a better way to handle the danger and rehearse that better way in preparation for the next time we face the danger. But after we establish and adequately rehearse a better strategy, there is no further benefit to reliving the danger. At this point the choice to continue dwelling on the fear, rather than filling our minds with Philippians 4:8 kinds of thoughts, can be sinful. In large measure we choose our thoughts, and we are exhorted to take every thought captive to Christ (2 Cor 10:5). That is a hard discipline to learn, but a necessary one. We are not to allow our minds to be filled with thoughts that are negative and serve no positive purpose.

On the other hand, sometimes after a dangerous and terrifying experience, these memories continue to come to us unbidden from time to time or even quite often. Psychologists refer to such unwelcome thoughts as "intrusive thoughts." Sometimes we have nightmares replaying these traumatic experiences, or flashbacks that may cause us to think we are in the situation again. This is not a matter of failing to choose good thoughts. Rather this is a matter of how the brain functions when traumatic memories have not been adequately worked through. The memories may be very piecemeal. Images flash through the brain. Sounds are heard. Sensations are felt. Feelings and thoughts are experienced, and any or all of these might be divorced from other parts of the memory.

These are symptoms of Post-Traumatic Stress Disorder. This is particularly likely to happen if you have been exposed to or been a victim of violence or threatened violence. If you have seen rebel troops close at hand, if you have been car-jacked, if you have suffered armed robbery, if you have been in a car accident and seen a family member deeply injured or killed, if you have been evacuated...How many things a missionary might experience that may create Post-Traumatic Stress Disorder! These retrospective fearful memories are not chosen. They push their way into consciousness unbidden, and they refuse to leave—or they return very quickly when banished.

If you are suffering from Post-Traumatic Stress Disorder, one of the most helpful things to do is tell someone the story. In telling the story you force your brain to move the images from the right side of the brain to the left side, which is the side used for language. In moving images to the language side of the brain, the different bits and pieces begin to come together, forming a whole memory instead of a piecemeal memory. It is important for the person listening not to judge and not to advise, but simply to listen, empathizing gently but not emoting much. In this kind of an atmosphere, you are likely to feel comfortable enough to tell your story as fully as possible. By relating your story, you help bring the pieces together and bring much healing to yourself. Intrusive memories, nightmares, and flashbacks are likely to become less frequent and less intense. If, however, these continue to occur and be troublesome, by all means consult a professional counselor. It is not at all unusual to need some professional help in overcoming the retrospective fears caused by the way our brains process traumatic experiences.

Present fear

Present danger is actually before us, and fear equips us to face it. Adrenaline is pumped into the blood stream, dramatically increasing our physical strength. Cortisol inundates our brain, and our thinking becomes very quick and focused. We are equipped to deal with the danger in an effective manner. This is the purpose for which God gave us the gift of fear.

Suppositional fear

This kind of fear can best be described as the many "What ifs ..." of life. The danger could happen but may not be likely. Yet we imagine it happening and feel the emotions that would accompany the danger if it did happen. Two common patterns of suppositional fear are described by the words "worry" and "anxiety." Worry is having something specific in mind and feeling fear while imagining the danger happening. Your son may have recently received his driving license, and you feel fear that he might have an accident each time he goes out in the car. Another example would be feeling fear of the discovery of cancer each time you visit the doctor, because it tends to run in your family. In each case, there is some specific danger that you think about, and by filling your mind with the possibility, you feel fearful even though the danger is not present at the moment and is not highly likely to happen.

Anxiety, on the other hand, is more general. It's not that you fear a possible accident involving your son at somewhat predictable times (when your son is driving the car), but you feel fearful that something bad is going to happen almost all the time.

Now there is good news and bad news about worry and anxiety. Let me give you the bad news first: God gave us the gift of fear to alert us to danger and to energize us for facing it. The adrenaline, cortisol and other biochemicals which he programmed to be released in abundance upon encountering danger actually do us harm when released continually. God intended for these biochemicals to flood our blood stream for several minutes up to a few hours. Our bodies should then return to normal for days and even weeks before experiencing another adrenaline surge. When these biochemicals are released for hours at a time several times a day or all day long, as happens with anxiety, the biochemical flood does us harm. We may develop ulcers, heart palpitations, asthma and other ailments. Please do not misunderstand: these illnesses are not always produced by anxiety. They have many other possible causes. However, it is well documented that, when we allow ourselves to experience constant anxiety, we bring about physical harm.

Now here's the "good news" about worry and anxiety. Because we live in a fallen world and bad things happen, sooner or later something bad will happen to you. When it does, you will already have adrenaline and cortisol racing through you and will be primed to tackle the danger—that is, if you haven't broken down from all those biochemicals wearing you out!

God did not intend for biochemicals to course through our blood stream often. They are resources meant to be saved until danger is present. Scripture exhorts us not to be anxious for a reason. To be fearful when confronted by danger is appropriate. However, it is not appropriate to be fearful often that something dangerous might come our way. It is a misuse of the gift of fear that God gave us.

Realistic fear

This is somewhat like anticipatory fear, except that we do not know for sure that the feared event will occur. It is very possible but not yet present and perhaps avoidable. This is a fear that alerts us to do our homework and make mental preparation in case the danger materializes. This is the purpose behind the fire drills we had in school. If a fire were to occur, everyone would know what to do. The practice drills happened often enough and usually unannounced so that, in the event of a real fire, people would probably stay calm and orderly. Realistic fears, then, do not paralyze us; they motivate us to form a plan and to practice that plan until it becomes familiar. This is an appropriate response to the gift of fear that God has given.

Fears of Western Female Missionaries in Islamic Cultures

Powerlessness under foreign law

Whether ministering through a creative access role or an approved activity, many missionaries in Islamic cultures have fairly narrow parameters in which to work. If government or religious officials perceive a violation of these parameters, the threat of deportation, imprisonment or persecution is very real. In many such cultures, the basic rule is that one is guilty until proven innocent. Whether falsely or justly accused, punishment for perceived violations may be swift, arbitrary, and without the benefit of a good defense attorney. Missionaries may be viewed as the enemy and treated as such. They may fear not only for themselves, but for their families, colleagues and national associates as well. They may face the danger of physical harm or the emotional chaos of being uprooted from their homes and ministries.

Sexual harassment and degradation

In Islamic cultures it is fairly common for men to harass, degrade, and exploit women. Their eyes freely undress women in public places. Their hands touch parts of the female's body that should be private. Their lewd comments and facial expressions degrade women. This can be intimidating to the female missionary, creating fear not only for herself, but also for her daughters. Experiences such as these go beyond the term "uncomfortable" or "embarrassing."

Because sexuality is such a deeply personal matter, this kind of harassment can go to the core of a woman's being, bringing about a deep sense of shame. Even though she has done nothing to provoke the behavior, she may feel as though she has lost some of her purity—a feeling similar to the sense that there is filth stuck to oneself after having been pushed into a trashcan. The female missionary can thus feel fear at the approach of a man who is likely to create danger to her emotional safety, bringing a sense of degradation and shame.

Loss of identity and significance

This is related to the fear produced by sexual harassment and degradation. Being treated as sexual objects for the amusement of men can deeply impact identity and values. Instead of having the confidence that comes from having been created in the image of God and redeemed and adopted by God, the female missionary and her daughters may feel like objects for men to look at and play with. Living in cultures in which women are seen as inferior to men with fewer rights and privileges, it is easy to begin to feel like a "nobody." It may be hard for a woman to remember that she is a daughter of the King of Kings and that this king values his daughters as much as he values his sons. She faces constant danger to her emotional well-being and her sense of significance. It is appropriate to be fearful about this danger.

Effect on children

Children may be affected by the sexual harassment that often exists in Islamic cultures. A low view of women can undermine a girl's self-confidence and positive sense of identity. It can also impact her attitudes toward sexuality. She might be ashamed to be a female. She might become promiscuous as a result of too much sexual attention too early in life. Or the opposite could happen—she could feel so negative about sexuality that it would be difficult for her to develop a normal sexual relationship with her husband upon getting married. These effects can be traced back to the sexual harassment of the Islamic culture in which the girl was reared. So these are other dangers to be feared: the danger to the emotional well-being of missionary daughters and the danger to some of the more intimate aspects of their daughters' marriages in the next generation.

But what about male missionary children? Are they affected as well? The answer is "yes." Growing up in an Islamic culture, it is possible that an MK would adopt the attitudes around him and develop a low view of women. This could affect the ways he interacts with his mother and sisters. It could affect his choice of a wife and his relationship with her, as well as his relationship with his daughters. This, too, is a danger to be faced—a danger to the quality of marriage and parenting in the next generation.

Reputation as a missionary

People want to see results. Mission boards and supporting churches may want positive numbers or statistics. Reputation is on the line, and sometimes support as well! Some missionaries have ministered for over a decade before being able to report the first convert. Are you afraid you might have the same experience? Are you afraid people will see you as a failure? Are you afraid your friendships will suffer? Are you afraid your support might decrease? These are common fears, fears of losing something that one values a great deal.

Spiritual warfare

Sometimes the sense of the Enemy's presence is almost palpable in those places where he has reigned unchallenged for centuries or even millennia. It can be frightening to invade his territory and suffer his opposition. Certainly no believer should attempt this carelessly or in his own strength. Although God has provided a full armor for our protection and the Enemy's ultimate defeat has already been secured, it nevertheless behooves every believer to be cautious in dealing with the Enemy. The danger is very real, and the right kind of fear can heighten one's alertness and energy. The right kind of fear (respect and caution, but not terror) is not a contradiction to knowing that greater is he who is in us than he who is in the world.

Dealing with Fear

Identify the danger

It is important to name the danger and size it up. Do not exaggerate the danger or your fear. But do not minimize them either. Sometimes we hear sayings such as, "I cried because I had no shoes, until I met a man who had no feet." This might be appropriate to quote to someone filled with self-pity, but in general it is not a helpful concept. Scripture tells us that they who compare themselves among themselves are not wise. You can always find someone worse off than you, and you can always find someone better off than you. That is not the point. The point is that your fear is realistic, and that it is important. Missionaries tend to minimize their emotions. They often belittle themselves for feeling afraid. I would encourage you not to do that. If your fear is valid—that is, if there is a danger to your physical, mental, emotional, or spiritual well-being—then fear is appropriate and is a gift from God to equip you to deal with the danger. But do not let yourself become panic-stricken in the face of danger. God will make a way for you, and he will bring good out of whatever happens. The danger is real, but so is God. Size up the danger, but also remember how big God is!

Take proactive measures

Determine what you can do to keep yourself and those you love as safe as possible. This may mean developing resources. It may mean devising a strategy to deal with specific, known, potential dangers. It may mean mentally rehearsing certain safety procedures or acting them out so they become "second nature." Proactive measures may mean developing a mission station plan, or a plan communicated to an MK school. Make every reasonable provision ahead of time for dealing with dangers you know to be realistic on the field on which you are serving.

Put the adrenaline and cortisol to good use

Upon feeling fear, your body releases goodly amounts of adrenaline, which creates physical strength and energy. Your body also releases cortisol, which brings mental alertness and quick thought. One of the difficulties of feeling fear when the feared event is not confronting us at the moment is that we are "all revved up with nowhere to go." Having nothing constructive on which to focus all this excess energy, we are likely to use it in ways that inadvertently hurt other people or create relational difficulties. Remember that basement you wanted to get cleaned out, or the fence you wanted to repair or your "spring cleaning" that has not yet been done? This is a good time! It is helpful to tackle something physical rather than something mostly mental (such as a computer project). It is important once the fear is identified to begin taking proactive measures to deal with it, and then to find a way to help all the excess energy dissipate.

Verbalize the fear to a trusted friend

It is important to express your fear with words and to share those words with a trusted friend. This friend needs to be chosen somewhat carefully, because not all friends are skillful listeners! Some friends tend to be long on advice and short on empathy, and that is the opposite of what is needed when dealing with fear. You need someone who can listen well, reflect back to you what you are saying, encourage you, and pray with you and for you. When you are sharing your fear with a friend, seek to do so without minimizing or apologizing for the fear (e.g., "I know I shouldn't feel this way, but ..."). State what the fear is, what the danger is behind the fear, and what you think you can do to prepare for the danger. Just as you should be careful not to minimize the fear, also be careful not to exaggerate it. Use your friend's reflections of what you are saying to help you "size up the fear" and determine whether you are seeing the danger in true proportion rather than minimizing or exaggerating it. After you and your friend have evaluated the fear in its true proportions, talk about proactive measures that can be taken, and then pray together. Burdens (and thus fears) that are shared are considerably easier to carry!

Acknowledge the timeliness of grace

God doesn't give grace ahead of schedule. If you are facing surgery, there is plenty of grace as you enter the hospital doors, but God does not give that same grace three weeks ahead of time as you allow fear to fill your mind ahead of schedule. When experiencing fear in an anticipatory way, decide on proactive measures, take them, and then choose to fill your mind with the kinds of thoughts described in Philippians 4:8. That is a choice. If you choose to dwell on your anticipatory fearful thoughts, you are likely to find that God's grace and peace elude you.

Seek the perspective of eternity

Colossians 3:1,2 exhorts us to "Set your minds on things above" and "Set your hearts on things above." When we are thinking God's thoughts and giving value to the things that God values, we can better take charge of our fears. The Lord Jesus admonished us not even to fear those who can kill the body but rather the one who can throw the soul into hell (Luke 12:4-12). With the perspective of eternity in mind, the things of this earth become less fearsome. 2 Corinthians 4:16-18 informs us that once we are "on the other side," even the worst things we have suffered in life will be seen as light and fleeting from the perspective of eternity. We need to remind ourselves that we belong to another kingdom, that we are just passing through, that our home is elsewhere, and that the values of that kingdom and our eternal home need to be the lens through which we view our temporal circumstances. As we choose to focus our minds and hearts on the things of God—the things of eternity—temporal dangers are likely to shrink substantially, and our fears along with them.

Put into practice Philippians 4:8

We are told in 2 Corinthians 10:5 to take charge of our thoughts, bringing them into subjection to the Lord Jesus Christ. This is something that most of us need to learn to do; it is not automatic. And Philippians 4:8 tells us what kinds of thoughts we must choose to fill our minds: "Whatever is true, whatever is noble, whatever is right, whatever is pure, whatever is lovely, whatever is admirable—if anything is excellent or praiseworthy—think about such things." In other words, we are to fill our minds with positive thoughts. Somewhere in this world God is doing something good and those are the kind of thoughts we need to be thinking. After identifying the danger behind the fear, taking constructive steps to prevent or manage it, acknowledging the sufficiency of God's grace at the moment of danger, and seeking the eternal perspective, all that remains is choosing to fill our minds with positive thoughts. We need to "change the channel" and focus on something positive that fits Philippians 4:8 kind of thinking. This is sometimes a difficult discipline, but it is necessary.

I remember the years in which my major goal was learning this spiritual discipline of taking every thought captive to Christ. I bought a watch that beeped every half hour or so. Every beep became a reminder to check my thoughts. Were they Philippians 4:8 thoughts or other thoughts? If they did not fit the Philippians 4:8 categories, then I chose to "change the channel" in my head. I had to choose positive thoughts. At first the channel remained in focus for only a minute or two, then it would drift to another channel. But as I consciously redirected my thoughts every half hour, they began to stay on the chosen channel a little longer before wandering off again. Slowly I began to gain more control of my thought life, choosing to bring my thoughts into captivity to Christ. It was not easy, and it did not happen quickly, but with consistent practice I got much better at maintaining the Philippians 4:8 "channel" in my mind.

If fear does not remit, seek help

As I said above, taking control of your thoughts takes practice. It is neither automatic nor learned quickly. However, with consistent practice you should be able to choose and maintain positive thoughts in your mind. When you learn to choose the Philippians 4:8 "channel" and maintain it, you will experience God's peace. The next verse, Philippians 4:9 confirms, "And the God of peace will be with you." The Old Testament version of this promise is Isaiah 26:3: "You will keep in perfect peace him whose mind is steadfast because he trusts in you." But what if, even after much practice, a person does not make progress in maintaining the Philippians 4:8 channel and gains no relief from agitation and fear?

Sometimes chemicals in the brain can be out of balance and result in fearful feelings. Even though a person with this kind of chemical imbalance makes every effort to control his thoughts and take an eternal perspective, he remains fearful and the peace of God, elusive. In this case, it would be important to seek professional help, just as a diabetic needs insulin to keep chemicals in the body in the right balance. People who have an imbalance in brain chemicals need the right medication to bring the right balance. This is not something of which to be ashamed, any more than one would be ashamed of taking insulin as a diabetic. It is a physiological problem that produces an emotional symptom—an inability to stop feeling fearful. If the problem is biochemical, spiritual disciplines will not help any more than they would help the diabetic survive without insulin or a broken bone to heal correctly without medical attention. Sometimes God does miracles and heals without medical intervention, but more often he uses the means he has made available to us. The inability to learn to control fearful feelings deserves the help of an expert to treat the brain chemistry that is probably imbalanced.

Please note that I did not begin with, "See a psychologist" as the first step! Although I am a Christian psychologist, I do not believe that everyone needs to see a psychologist, and I don't believe that seeing a psychologist is usually the best place to start. There are many things that you can do for yourself and ways that you can utilize the community of believers, the Body of Christ, to deal with your feelings of fear. But if you have tried the various steps and do not see reasonable progress after an adequate period of time, the reason may be biochemical. It could also be something in your background that is blocking the peace of God. When you have tried your best to put into practice what you know to do and you still do not experience God's peace, look for a professional whom God has provided to assist you in finding out what is wrong.

Conclusion

To the degree that we adequately and accurately bear God's image, we experience emotion because he is a God of deep passion. We experience both the positive emotions—those that were very fitting in the Garden of Eden—and the so-called "negative emotions," those that help equip us for dealing with the difficulties of life outside of Eden. All of these negative emotions serve a purpose; and the purpose of fear is to alert us to the presence of danger and to equip us to face danger.

When we feel fear, adrenaline floods our body and gives physical strength, energy, and stamina. Cortisol floods our brain and gives us mental alertness and quickness of mental response. God gave these to us as a way to help us face the dangers of life outside of Eden. But God intended that adrenaline and cortisol and other such biochemicals be used sparingly, only in the face of immediate danger. When we think about danger, however, our body begins releasing these chemicals, even though there is no danger present—only thoughts about danger.

Here is a curious thought. Did you know that your brain does not distinguish between reality and imagination? That's why, when you watch a scary movie, your heart starts beating faster. If the scary part lasts more than a few seconds, you may find that your hands become clenched into tight fists, your breathing becomes more rapid, and you might even begin perspiring. The conscious part of your mind knows that you are sitting safely in the privacy of your own living room. But an unconscious part of your mind cannot distinguish between reality and fiction. As you expose your senses to the sights and sounds on television, the unconscious part of your mind interprets the input as real danger and prepares your body to deal with the danger by increasing your heart rate and pouring adrenaline into your blood stream.

So it is with your fearful thoughts. As you dwell on whatever you fear, the images, sounds and other sensory perceptions you create in your mind cause the unconscious part of your mind to think the danger is actually at hand. Your brain doesn't know the difference between your imagining danger and danger actually being present. As you think about the danger, you become a walking pharmacy!

God intended for you to have these chemical highs infrequently, only when danger is actually confronting you. Because the constant barrage of these chemicals in your system begins to do harm, you develop physical difficulties. You begin to feel shaky. Your strength begins to wane. Your body needs increasingly larger doses of adrenaline to give the strength needed to deal with danger—real or imagined. Your body begins to break down from the constant chemical highs that your fearful thoughts bring on.

So how do you stop that from happening? Evaluate the danger. How big is the danger and how likely is it to happen? Do whatever you can to prevent it or to prepare to deal with it effectively. As you give thought to it, adrenaline and cortisol are likely to increase, so use these for a good purpose. If you don't, they are likely to push you to do something inappropriate that you might regret. Use the excess energy constructively by talking with a friend who will listen well and pray with you. Look at the possible danger in light of eternity's values. Then choose to put all thought of this danger aside and focus on the good things of this life and the good things that God is doing. If, with practice, you are not able to do this consistently, seek professional help to find out what is blocking God's peace in your life.

May God help us all to value the gift of fear that he has given us. May he help us face realistic dangers with careful preparation and empower us to keep our minds stayed on him and on the things of eternity, so that his peace will dwell in us. May we learn to commit all our cares to him, taking burdens to him in prayer, so that his perfect peace will garrison both our hearts and our minds until the Day of Jesus Christ.

Dr. Jeanne Jensma has been the Director of Counseling for four years at ALONG-SIDE, a ministry of restoration and refreshment for missionaries. Jeanne has a passion for promoting growth and wholeness in Christ in missionaries in order to help maximize the effectiveness of their ministries. Jeanne spent over a decade in Brazil as a missionary before serving at ALONGSIDE.

A Testimony of Dealing with Fear: Confessions of a Wimp

by Karol Downey

Do you remember the Hefty trash bag commercial—the one with the name-brand bag that could hold anything and was described as "hefty, hefty, hefty"? Then there was the off-brand of trash bag that would tear as it was being lifted—you would hear this voice saying, "Wimpy, wimpy, wimpy." If we were to divide missionaries into these two categories: the hefty ones who seem as if they could handle anything and everything, and the wimpy ones who are weak and fragile, I would definitely fall into the wimpy category!

Heading to our candidate school in 1985, the closer we got to its location, the sicker my stomach felt. I knew my life was going to drastically change forever and I was scared. After being accepted by the mission and before going overseas, I would grow fearful and very nervous as I thought about what the future might hold. Would I be able to learn a new language? Would I be able to make it? When I read about the mighty women missionaries of faith like Elisabeth Elliot, Amy Carmichael, and Isobel Kuhn, I wondered how I could join the ranks of those called missionaries.

Friends in my husband's hometown near Chicago would ask us, "How can you take your children to terrorist-filled countries?" "This will be so dangerous!" "How can you live in such a perilous place?" A seed of fear would take root in my soul and start to grow as I wondered if we would be hijacked on our way overseas, or if my children would be at risk of a terrorist attack. The funny thing was that when we arrived overseas our Arab friends would ask my husband where he was from, and when he replied Chicago, they would be aghast. They would say, "How could you live in Chicago? What a dangerous place! You can't even open up a store there without a gangster coming in to rob you! We could never live there!"

I do remember being concerned for my family before we left the United States. Will there be adequate health care for my children when they are sick? Where will they go to school? While I am gone, what might happen to my family that I am leaving behind?

As we landed overseas and I began my missionary career, all the things I had worried about and had been afraid of seemed groundless. The people were friendly. There was a school and childcare for my children. There were good doctors and hospitals available. Language study was difficult, but not impossible. I also figured out that I didn't have to compare myself with missionary legends; I could be myself and keep walking with the Lord and let him use me as he willed.

But once those fears diminished, there were others ready to take their place. What if we got kicked out of the country? What if the person talking to me and asking me questions is really an informant for the secret police? What if my husband goes to jail? One of the few times he went in for questioning, he didn't get home until 1:00 A.M. My nerves were frayed and I wanted to run somewhere I could feel safe; but as I drew near to the Lord, he was there. I wasn't as afraid as I thought I would be years ago when I had wondered about this possibility. Once the questioning had actually happened, it was over. My fear focused more on the unknown. What would tomorrow bring? What would lie ahead as a result of this happening today?

Various questions attacked me. What if no one ever comes to know the Lord because of my ministry? What if others think I am a failure and drop our support? What if I am a failure? What if someone does trust Christ and then suffers for it? What if my kids are emotionally scarred because of a less than perfect social environment or school situation? How much damage does a teacher do when she pulls continuously on a little boy's ear or threatens to throw him out of the window if his homework isn't turned in on time? What if my children suffer long-term physical hurts because of their bouts with dysentery and exposure to disease? What if I go out to visit my friend and a man does more than proposition me or touch me? What if I run into another taxi driver who tries to fondle my breasts while I try to get away from him?

As God helped me deal with each of those fears, he used the principle of faith. Fear and faith are opposites. You cannot be walking by faith and in fear at the same time. Fear concentrates on the future, the "what ifs" of life. Faith focuses on our sovereign, loving God—the loving Father who is totally in control over everything that enters our lives and who uses each event to ultimately bring us good and glory to himself. When I would feel fear start to rise as I thought about our future, I would be reminded that I must trust in him in the present.

When we returned to live and minister in the States in 1998, I thought I had worked through almost all of my fear issues. We were going to be living in America. What could possibly happen in the safety of my own home country?

It was the summer of 1999 when my husband's brother passed away suddenly, at the age of 49, from a heart attack. I quickly remembered my husband's dad had died at the age of 46 from the same thing. I looked at my husband who was 42—what if he died and left me?

As he wanted to talk through insurance issues, different decisions about the practical ramifications of death, I wanted to flee. I cried as I told him I didn't want to talk about it. He asked me one night what I wanted him to say to help me. I told him to tell me that he wasn't going to die and leave me. I was, so to speak, "scared to death."

Again God lovingly called me to quit being afraid and to trust him moment by moment, day by day. It is impossible to let fear rule in my heart and to trust God at the same time!

I think most of our fears—as women, as Christians, as missionaries—are focused on the "what ifs" of life, the unknowns of the future, all of the things we lack control over. Feeling fear is normal. But when fear makes its home in our hearts and rules our lives, God lovingly confronts us with the question, "Will you trust me today?"

Instead of worrying about the future and fearing what it may hold, we could direct our energy toward trusting God today. Faith develops through the exercise of that faith—trusting God through each of life's adventures.

In the trash bag example of life, I don't want to be "wimpy, wimpy, wimpy" in my faith. But if I focus on the "what ifs" of tomorrow and the concerns I cannot control, there is no faith, only fear. Psalm 56:3-4 says, "When I am afraid, I will trust in you. In God, whose word I praise, in God I trust; I will not be afraid. What can mortal man do to me?" It is only as I decide to trust him moment by moment in whatever comes my way that I can, through faith become "hefty, hefty, hefty"!

Karol Downey worked with her husband in the Middle East for twelve years and is now working at her mission agency's home office.

Challenges for Singles on the Mission Field

by Laili

What challenges does a single face on the mission field? This is a legitimate question that is asked often of me. When I'm on the field, my single status does not fit the world view of those to whom I minister. Their question is simply: "Why aren't you married?" Regardless of our state or station in life, all of us face challenges on the mission field such as stress, loneliness and the lack of a support system. However, struggles more particular to the unmarried worker include the unfavorable social stigma of being single, the absence of a ministry partner, limited ministry opportunities and lack of recognition.

Unfavorable social stigma

It is not uncommon for those in our target audiences to make one or more negative presuppositions about the single female missionary: she has something wrong with her, physically or otherwise, which renders her unmarketable; she must be an immoral person who prefers not to be married in order to support her lifestyle; or perhaps she is just weird and does not recognize the value of having children. My target audience is not as merciless with their probing as other audiences, but those of us who are single still must manage their presuppositions. How then do we begin to manage and triumph?

The most important and basic step is to accept being single, at least for the time being. Learn to be content, appreciating the benefits of being a single (1 Cor 7:32-35). At least half of the battle is won when a single comes to this point of acceptance and contentment; then the issue of not being married—and the endless questions regarding it—will become less of a mental and emotional handicap. When singles learn to enjoy their blessed singleness, I believe their faith in God's provision deepens and becomes more real.

However, coming to terms with singleness does not decrease the many questions from a target audience. Other pro-active steps are needed to slowly dispel presuppositions and establish the missionary's reputation as a godly single woman. The second step, then, is to live a lifestyle that is above reproach. We must be careful never to appear overly friendly toward the opposite sex. Innocent interaction with men may be construed as an indication of an immoral character. Living a careful lifestyle, however, results in the blessing of a godly and pure reputation. When questions arise about singleness, they are opportunities to share faith in God and his sufficiency to provide.

Absence of a ministry partner

The issue of loneliness is very real to both married and single missionaries. For singles who live without a roommate and minister without a partner, the loneliness may be more acute. There is no easy solution to this, but some of the following ideas might be considered:

- Work with other single women on the team.
- Work with married women on the team, many of whom cannot minister together with their husbands in most of the targeted audiences.
- Schedule social occasions with married women on the team to chat and share. Those who are mothers often feel isolated and long for more relational time with other women on the team.
- Form relationships with women from other Christian organizations.
- Pray and ask God to give you at least one significant national friend to mentor.

Limited ministry opportunities

The ministries of single female missionaries are limited to certain social groups. Married missionary women most often reach married women. Male missionaries minister to men. In fact everyone is limited because no one person can reach all strata of society. Understanding that God brings together teams of different people with various gifts to do his multi-pronged task can change limitations into opportunities. Given the immensity of the work at hand, plenty of ministry opportunities are available.

Lack of recognition as a single

A single might be prepared for lack of recognition from her target audience, particularly in societies which view child rearing as a woman's primary func-

tion; but she will be gravely disheartened if she receives the same signals from her married team members. One of the following solutions may be considered:
- Pray for acceptance and recognition, especially from the target audience, but be patient. This takes time.
- Gently bring your concerns to the attention of your team members, if the lack is on one's team. "Carefront" the team members if it persists. If necessary, confide in the field council or home office.

What I have shared, though by no means exhaustive, affirms that we are not alone in our challenges and that we can triumph, be content and actually have fun being singles. God is more than able to provide for our needs.

Laili has worked in Central Asia since 1997. She continues to minister among university women students and women in her neighborhood.

Singleness and Ministry to Muslim Women

by Melinda Hale

I have been in Muslim ministry for nine years with five and a half spent working in Central Asia. The flexibility and mobility of being single has enabled me
to bond with the culture in incredible ways. I lived with a local family for the
first six months and became their "daughter," attending every family event and
holiday. Most importantly, my singleness has enabled me to follow the example
of Jesus and demonstrate a revolutionary lifestyle.

Jesus was single in a culture where men were expected to marry. I wonder
how many Jewish mothers were trying to fix him up with their daughters? How
many young women were madly in love with him because he was the first man
who treated them with love and respect? Yet in the midst of all that, Jesus lived
a sinless, pure and holy life. He focused on the purposes of God, did what his
Father showed him and had wonderful relationships with people who were
married, single, old and young alike. His life was full of joy and was a blessing
to those around him.

Single women in Muslim ministry have the privilege of demonstrating that
wholeness and joy is not dependent upon marital status or motherhood. Joy
and wholeness in life come directly from a relationship with Jesus! This revolutionary concept, when lived out among Muslims, crumbles false spiritual
assumptions.

Challenges to Revolutionary Living

However, the single lifestyle in ministry to Muslim women is not without its
challenges. Cultural differences, spiritual forces of darkness and other obstacles block our way. Perhaps the most difficult are those that come from within.

The loss of identity

Prior to our missionary careers, some of us were business women or students. We were daughters and friends. We participated in or led small groups and taught Sunday school classes. Who are we now? Our roles have changed so drastically and, even if we know how to describe them in our new langauge, we probably sound like two-year-olds.

Missionary families also face these cultural changes but do so while maintaining their closest relationships. Singles face it alone. For some singles, this loss of structure and support is very hard. The foreign culture awaits with a double barrel shotgun of rejection. In one barrel rejection comes because unmarried women are not valued in the foreign world view. The second barrel is loaded with suspicion: were we kicked out from our families; are we spies, prostitutes or lesbians? Such unspoken negative messages about our identity can result in insecurity, discouragement and even depression.

We must continually ask ourselves questions related to our sense of identity. Is my identity secure in Christ? Do I know who I am in him? Does my head knowledge reach my heart, where it will sustain me through the difficult years of adjustment?

The need for relationships

We must have intimate relationships on the field. We need friends to hold us accountable and friends who know how to speak the truth. We need safe people with whom we can be honest about our joys and struggles and with whom we can confess sin. We need people with whom we can be vulnerable. And yet, for some missionaries, building relationships with teammates has been one of the greatest struggles.

We've all come to Christ at different stages in our lives and from many different backgrounds. One thing is sure: the enemy will attack us at our weakest points. These weak points are often related to past hurts in relationships with family, friends and even God. These issues must be addressed. Jesus wants to heal the broken parts of our hearts and the broken relationships in our lives, preferably before they explode in some isolated part of the Muslim world with little support.

Finding relational support and making our needs known takes initiative. We can't sit back and wait for a teammate to notice. Married people, especially, have so many concerns with spouses, kids and ministry that the needs of single teammates can easily be overlooked. Don't take it as a personal rejection.

Accept this as life on the field and take the initiative to share your life with them.

Our potential needs and struggles as singles in Muslim ministry are many: loneliness, restricted social lives, lack of male friendships, housing and room-mate decisions and, of course, the "how and when" of finding a mate (for those who do want to marry one day). We need friends on the field who can give us counsel and prayer support. Primarily we look to other women to be that sup-port. The friendship of our brothers in Christ is a great blessing, but we should take care to keep healthy boundaries and not develop inappropriate emotion-al intimacy. When I was on the field, I worked with the men on my team daily in our tentmaking roles. However I always made it a priority to develop as deep a relationship with their wives as I had with them. This kept the relationships healthy and balanced, leaving no room for jealousy.

We also need to be concerned for the cultural boundaries between the sexes. How we live, dress and interact with men will paint a picture for the local Muslim women of who we are and what we are like. We need to be careful that the image they see is the one we are trying to project. The assumption is prob-ably that most Western women (including Christians) are immoral, so we must go the extra mile to demonstrate a life of purity and devotion to God.

Jesus also blesses us with the joy of having Muslim women as friends. Deep friendships can develop when we are vulnerable and share our lives. Many Muslim women have few people they can trust but will often open their hearts and innermost secrets to us. Jesus wants to meet them at their place of need through me and through you.

The inevitability of suffering

Most North Americans have never faced suffering like the rest of the world; yet, according to Scripture, it is normal to the Christian life. Likely none of us have put our lives at risk by deciding to follow Christ. But life in the Muslim world is often filled with heartbreaking stories of suffering. Whether it is war, abuse, poverty, sickness or abandonment, the Muslim women we meet have lived through things we can't even imagine. We must be prepared with a solid belief in the goodness of God to face horrendous circumstances.

Suffering will also happen to us. The devil doesn't play fairly. At times I feel that being single in the Muslim world is itself a type of suffering. I long for mar-riage but, at forty, I am still single. Yet God is still good! Our suffering reminds us that we are indeed broken clay pots, but his light shines through our broken-ness and suffering, and the Muslims around us will see and be amazed.

The need for spiritual growth

How will we grow deeper in love with Jesus when all of our spiritual support structures are gone? There is no singles class, no Christian radio, no church fellowship like we are used to. The lack of these supports can either be an obstacle, or an opportunity to explore different spiritual disciplines—fasting, silence, meditating on Scripture, spiritual retreats and different styles of worship. Find out what refreshes you and inspires you in the Spirit, and let God use it to fill you up! He can do it, even in lands that are spiritual deserts. We can trust God as David did, "I know the Lord is always with me. I will not be shaken, for He is right beside me" (Psalm 16:8, NLT).

Having a strong team of intercessors is key to thriving on the field. We need a team of people with whom we can stay in close contact and share the nitty-gritty struggles and joys that we face. Knowing your intercessors are standing with you can make a significant difference during hard times.

There are other struggles for singles in Muslim ministry; but I believe that if we are secure in these four areas, we will be able to thrive, not just survive on the field. God is worthy and will give us all the grace we need to walk the path he has marked out for us. Whether we are single for one more week, or single until he takes us home, Psalm 16:11 is true, "You will show me the way of life, granting me the joy of your presence and the pleasures of living with you forever" (NLT). The road with Jesus is indeed the path of life!

Melinda Hale has worked for five and a half years in Central Asia doing church planting among Muslims. She is currently working in the U.S., training and equipping others to work with Muslim women.

Raising Radiant Daughters in Dark Places

by Emily J. van Dalen

PART 1: Dispelling the Silence

I can see the scene as clearly as a snapshot. The yellow-gray Asian sky is weighted with its own peculiar blend of smells . . . thick exhaust fumes, dust, cow-dung and spicy vegetable fritters from stalls beside the road. Bus horns blast over the drone of rickshaw motors as an excited gaggle of sixteen-year-old girls hurry by on a rare shopping trip to the city thirty miles away from the boarding school.

In the midst of the business . . . just for an instant, everything stands still. An indelible event imprints itself in my mind. A girlfriend and I are just rounding a corner in the crowded marketplace, when out of nowhere a bicycle veers toward us and a man jeeringly reaches out and grabs my friend's breast. Unbelievably the two of us walk on without even a break in our step. Our conversation continues with careful nonchalance. And never, not in over twenty-five years, has it been mentioned between us.

Perhaps I should place this incident in the context of a number of mental snapshots, a photo album that stays at the bottom of the drawer and is never shown to anyone. It stores the photos that didn't turn out quite right, complete with every stare, inappropriate touch, rude gesture and comment. It's the album of shame for young, vulnerable, Western females who live in an Islamic culture, and the photos are distorted with lies about what it means to be a woman.

But there were good memories too: the happiness of foreign words, textures and tastes flowing through my blood, heaping my life with good, non-American, wonderfully MK thoughts and feelings. I have so much thankfulness and joy in remembering. These along with the hard and damaging times reflect my experience.

In new generations of missionary families, perhaps there are ways in which some of that damage can be prevented. Let's start by looking at the silence that wedged itself so tightly between my friend and me. It speaks mutely of resignation and denial. It shrugs its shoulders and ducks its head and kicks at the dirt. What are some of the lies the silence validates? I believe they include the following:

Distortion of the female identity

"There is something wrong with being a woman; there is something wrong with me." Feelings of shame are not unusual for girls growing up in traditional Islamic cultures. Even though a child may be nurtured in a loving, Christian home, she lives in a setting in which she is constantly barraged with ungodly messages about her female identity. In traditional Islamic societies women are viewed as intrinsically inferior beings. The sacred written traditions in Islam (the Hadith) present women as spiritually, physically, intellectually and morally deficient. Their physical attractions are an irresistible and potentially dangerous entrapment for men.

These messages about womanhood can be profoundly confusing to MK girls. They see women walking behind men. They see them veiled and hidden behind walls. Their Muslim girlfriends are the last in their families to get food at mealtimes and the last to receive medical help when ill. Sometimes they may even be beaten and abused. When they were born, their reception as baby girls was often one of silence and disappointment.

To make things even more complicated, MK girls also experience negative input regarding their Western identity. As foreigners, they experience "curiosity harassment," hearing comments about their funny yellow hair or weird blue eyes. Western media transmits vivid images of women to Islamic viewers who assume that all Westerners are of the same character as those they see on televison. MK girls consequently become "fair game." As early as age eight or nine, even when completely covered in culturally appropriate attire, they are subject to jeers and inappropriate touching. They sense that this harassment is specifically sexual in nature. It aims at disparagement. It says, "You are contemptible. You deserve to be treated like a slut."

It is not surprising, then, that MK girls from these settings can grow up despising themselves. Among my acquaintances are women ranging in age from 20 to 60, many of whom silently agonize with doubts about their value and personhood. I'm convinced that at least some of it is rooted in years of disparagement and sexual harassment that was never recognized or acknowledged.

Dismissal of sexual harassment

"Sexual harassment occurs with such frequency that it is a non-event and should be ignored." This silent and completely false assumption infers that harassment is so commonplace, it must simply be endured. Like the ants, heat and dust, sexual harassment is supposedly just one more adaptation to be made within the culture. However, in his book, *The Wounded Heart* (NavPress, copy. 1990, Colorado Springs, CO), Christian psychologist Dan Allender, addresses the issues of childhood sexual abuse, stating that any kind of inappropriate sexual contact or interaction with a child causes damage. The longer the negative interactions continue the deeper the long-term effects.

One response that MK girls sometimes hear from adults after an incident is, "Just ignore it!" But the underlying message of this response may be understood as another way of saying, "Get used to it for goodness sake! What's wrong with you that you haven't yet adapted to this culture?" Another message is "This incident is so insignificant that it should be perfectly possible for you not to even notice that it happened." This kind of response makes the child's feelings of fear, indignation and humiliation inappropriate, rather than the abuse that happened against her. How, then, would the child respond to the adult? With silence—silence that comes from being discounted.

Development of fatalism

"There is no point in talking, because nothing will ever change." Whether she realizes it or not, a girl growing up as an MK in an Islamic culture is engaged in a battle for hope in a quagmire of fatalism. The fatalism draws its roots from two primary sources. The first is embedded in the Islamic belief system: Allah, the supreme and holy one, has ordained that the female is subservient to the male. To an MK growing up in this environment, it may appear that sexual harassment is an inevitable and justifiable consequence of being born female. There is no point in complaining. It is simply her fate.

The second type of fatalism an MK might experience relates to the call of God. She may postulate that, if God called her parents to a culture in which she is relentlessly harassed and degraded, her personal well-being is not as important to God as his "program" for the world. There is no point in asking him to do anything to change the situation. To speak up or complain would be to resist God's plan.

How do you arm a child to do battle with this two-pronged undercurrent of fatalism? How can you convey the message that change is possible? How can you convince her that being a girl is something to celebrate and that wonderful possibilities fill her future? It is vitally important to do open battle with the myths of powerlessness and fatalism. When we resign ourselves to the harassment and abuse of our little girls, we give in to the lie that God heartlessly calls people to serve him in ways that deeply and inevitably damage their children.

Fear of accusation

"If I talk about it, I'll be the one who gets the blame." This type of silence comes from the fear of accusation. At first glance it is plain to all of us that the blame for any kind of inappropriate sexual exchange lies fully with the perpetrator. But in the throes of frustration, confusion and shock, we adults sometimes are tempted to lash out at those nearest to us and least likely to resist. We can't confront an unseen hand that has dared to touch our daughter, so in the heat of the moment we turn on her instead. "What were you doing walking on that side of the street? Why can't you just watch where you're going?" In our helplessness to vent our fury against a huge and nameless cultural reality, we turn on the little face closest to us.

It's easy to do and understandable that it sometimes happens, but please don't do it. Your child will learn from your anger. She'll learn to be angry as well—angry with herself for being female and vulnerable; angry with her body for somehow inviting an attack; angry with parents who made decisions which placed her in a difficult culture; and angry with God for not protecting and cherishing her. And she'll learn to hold that anger in silence, because instinct tells her that a protest or response could quite possibly result in more blame.

What would be a response that honors God? Recognizing the truth and placing blame where it belongs is crucially important in the battle against silence. Openly name the violation against your child. Comfort her by being appropriately angry along with her. Discuss the incident, how she felt about it, and how God feels about it. Finally think together about possible options for doing things a little differently to avoid another incident.

Too busy to listen

"Why talk? I won't be heard." Sometimes this statement isn't a lie. So much has been said about the pressures of ministry overseas and the cost to the family. Yet often we still don't "get it." We act as though God will take care

of our responsibilities if we burn out doing his work. That is not how it works. Just as God's ministry is in and through his family, the Trinity and the Church, our ministries are in and through our families. Just as God listens to the prayers of his people, interceding and intervening for them, so we must take the time to listen to the secret heartaches and concerns of our children. Your daughter needs to know that when she is with you, she is in a place of trust, where she can find comfort and protection. She needs to be raised in a home where listening to one another is a part of the air that is breathed.

As I write this article my heart is torn in two directions. I write it as both a child and a parent. On the one side, I see myself as the little girl who climbed guava trees, flew kites, and played deliciously dusty games of marbles lying flat on her stomach, bare feet waving in the air. I see her as a bewildered adolescent who sensed an uneasy change in her world. I see her confusion, walking through the marketplace, eyes lowered. I see the man in the alley brushing past her too closely or the boy at the window rudely bursting into song. I remember the suggestive smiles, stares and touches.

On the other hand, I also see myself as the missionary mom. I remember the pleas for God's grace and strength and forgiveness as we raised three children in an urban, Islamic environment. How hard it was to stay deeply connected to each other as a family in the midst of so many ministry opportunities, mission responsibilities and political upheavals. How difficult it was to think of my children's emotional and spiritual needs when yet another curfew was announced, or the electricity faltered or the supply of boiled and filtered drinking water ran out. I remember the guilt feelings as I plunked my little girl in front of a video so that I could get just one more load of laundry done or one more e-mail answered.

So when the small hand tugs incessantly at my shirttail, I know the effort it takes to stop, look my daughter squarely in the face and listen when she says, "Look! Look at what is happening. Do you see? Do you care?" I know how hard it is for mission agencies in the midst of their visions and strategies, programs and personnel, crises and budget crunches, to stop, take time, kneel down, look directly in the faces of the little ones they are sending overseas, and say, "I see you. I hear you."

Truly seeing and truly caring for these little ones takes time and effort and thoughtful preparation. But I believe that pro-active intervention in the lives of these girls is far more crucial now than it has ever been before. During my growing up years, many Islamic regions of the world were more pragmatic in both religion and politics. Returning to the field as an adult eleven years later, I was astonished at the change in Islamic practice! The dress was far more conservative. The observance of the month of fast was no longer a matter of personal choice. The study of the Arabic language and the beliefs of Islam were mandated in all public schools.

At the same time as the shift towards conservatism is taking place among many Islamic nations, Christian mission agencies are making increasingly concerted efforts to penetrate these less-reached Islamic peoples and cultures. Growing numbers of missionary families are raising their children in increasingly rigid Islamic societies. The need, therefore, to talk openly about sexual harassment and abuse in that context is urgent. There must be specific, clearly-focused research on the impact that growing up in Islamic cultures has on young girls. Wise, sensitive and godly strategies for raising daughters in these cultures should be discussed and taught to parents and other care givers.

God continues to call us to serve him in Islamic countries. When we do so, we are engaged in a battle between darkness and light, lies and Truth. One of those lies tells our daughters, "You are of no value. I can treat you however I like." Our willingness to resolutely engage that lie and expose it, to raise radiant daughters in dark places, is a reflection of the glory of the One whom we serve. May our daughters deeply know that they are children of the Light.

Part II: Telling the Truth

Radiance. Isn't that what we long to see when we look in the faces of our daughters? We want to see the celebration of heart that happens when a girl knows to the core of her being that she is made in the "image of God." We want her to know that when God created her, he cupped her tenderly in his hands and laughed over her in delight.

As our daughters grow up in Islamic cultures, how can we pro-actively offset the negative input—the comments, the stares, the frequent small abuses that teach untruthful messages about women? I believe we can only do it by seeking every possible means of reaffirming the Truth. We must effectively communicate to our daughters that they are of value, that their accomplishments are significant, that God loves them dearly.

Why is this such a difficult thing to do in practice? In the crush of ministry responsibilities, under the pressure of trying to live a culturally sensitive lifestyle, in the crazy, unpredictable patterns of our life overseas, it may be difficult to take the time to see, hear, touch and love our daughters. Where are we to find the resources to replenish in them what gets so terribly depleted by the negative messages they absorb? How can we reach through and fill the hearts of our daughters with good?

I wonder if part of our difficulty lies in the tension we feel between living "incarnationally" within the culture and, at the same time, resisting its ungodly Islamic view of women. To what extent are we to follow the cultural norms, and at what point should we take a stand against them? If we take a stand against them, should we do it only verbally, or should we do it by making lifestyle changes with regard to how we raise our daughters?

Somehow Jesus handled these hard issues so well. He was able to reach straight through cultural barriers and speak to women soul to soul. He didn't just do it with words; he didn't just do it in all the socially acceptable ways. In fact, the Jesus we follow into these Islamic cultures is unpredictable and upsetting. He doesn't always stick to the rules. He goes to radical lengths to become incarnate and to fully identify with those he comes to save. And then, having done that, he promptly breaks the cultural norms, sits down beside a well and engages a Samaritan woman in personal conversation. Or he allows a harlot to touch his feet with her tears. He shocks and alienates people and then goes out searching for them, one lost sheep at a time.

What would this same Jesus do in our position in an Islamic context? How does he want his women to live in such a culture? Which cultural norms concerning women would he accept and which would he denounce? What truths would he want us to know as we seek to raise the daughters He has given us?

The truth about attitudes towards women and sexuality

Jesus never minimized the truth about sin. He knew there were things terribly wrong with the world and he talked about those things. Sometimes when we enter another culture, we make the mistake of bending over backwards to adapt. We don't want to appear as though we are in culture shock or that we are being culturally insensitive. We focus so hard on becoming like those we have come to serve, that we forget to focus on becoming more like Jesus and relating to others with uncompromising godliness. We focus on blending in with the culture, and ignore ungodly aspects that we should be facing head on.

"Tim" and "Cheryl," a young expatriate couple settled in our city overseas. Because they had taken pre-field courses on linguistics, world religions and cross-cultural relationships, they thought they were well prepared, but there were some things they hadn't anticipated. Their assumption was that in an

Islamic country, a man would never stare at or touch a woman inappropriately. So the first time Cheryl was pinched she was dumbfounded. She thought she'd imagined it. The next time it happened, she knew she hadn't! She turned indignantly to Tim expecting him to defend her. Unfortunately, he was still stuck in his pre-arrival assumptions about how women were treated. It became a real stress in their marriage. When something happened, he would tell her she was imagining things, being oversensitive or exaggerating. Once or twice he even made the mistake of joking about it. For a while their marriage went through a rough time because of his blindness toward the culture.

One of the very first things we must do when we enter a new culture is to open our eyes wide and take a good look around. Acknowledge the truth. What is the reality of life here? What is the status of women? What are the local beliefs and practices related to human sexuality? I've already mentioned that sexual harassment of women is common in many Islamic countries. Now look around you again. What are some of the other forms of sexual interaction? In one Islamic country a common form of teasing little boys is pulling their genitals. How can you prepare your son for this? In a number of South and East Asian countries it is an acceptable practice to masturbate infants to soothe them or help them sleep. Is this an issue you need to discuss with the care givers that watch your children? In some Islamic countries polygamy is still acceptable. What will you teach your children about this? In other places caste groupings within the social structure engage in transvestitism. Men dressed as women may approach your child and beg for money. How will you explain that to her?

Not all these things happen in every country. I give them as examples of things that do happen in various Islamic cultures. It is crucially important to learn what happens in your culture and to prepare your family for living in that context.

One of the best ways to counter the lies your daughter experiences in relation to her sexual identity is to give her a thorough grounding in what the Bible teaches. Your daughter, even at a very young age, needs to know the wonder and joy of being created female. Many good Christian books and materials on sex education are available for all age levels. Focus on the Family is a good resource. NavPress has an excellent series of four books, written by Stan & Brenna James, for ages 3 through 14, *God's Design for Sex* (NavPress, 1995. Colorado Springs, CO). *It's Okay to Say No!* (Preschool Press, Playmore Inc. & Waldman Pub. Corp., New York) is a helpful coloring book that teaches about "good touching" and "bad touching."

A helpful guideline many parents teach their kids is that any part of the body covered by a swimsuit is private and belongs only to you. It is "out of bounds" for anyone else. Talk with your children about what they should do if these boundaries are violated in any way. Let them know they are allowed to say "no," even to adults and that they are to move away from the person and report the incident to their parents or other trusted adult care givers.

Sexual molestation and abuse is far more common on the mission field than most of us think. Most often the perpetrators aren't strangers but are people that are known or trusted. Significant numbers of MKs have been molested by beloved household helpers or by members of the "mission family," When the abuse is perpetrated by someone in intimate relationship with the family, it can resemble incest, and the resulting damage is even deeper.

Entrusting our children to someone else's care is a necessary part of life. It would be wrong to raise our children in an environment of fear and suspicion. It would be wrong for our children to never interact deeply with adults in the community. Where we need to be careful, however, is with *implicit* trust—trust which is absolute or unquestioning. We must be wise and discerning, soberly acknowledging that abuse can and does happen in any kind of circumstance. Aware of the symptoms and signs of abuse, we ought to create a home environment where a child is heard no matter what questions or issues are raised.

The following safeguards can be built into the routines of our lives overseas and will help prevent opportunities for abuse.

Establish wise baby-sitting practices and guidelines. Never leave children with baby-sitters unless you know them well, and even then, be cautious. Call home or check back unexpectedly during your absence to make sure everything is all right. Teach teenage babysitters not to give unnecessary information on the phone and not to let the caller know that there is no adult in the home.

Be thorough in screening household helpers. After hiring a helper, re-train them thoroughly according to your values and standards of behavior. Explain to them in detail what is and what is not acceptable behavior.

Be involved in your child's school. Make sure the school (especially if it is a boarding school) has thorough screening procedures as well as oversight and accountability for staff. Be

involved; get to know the staff; be aware of your child's responses
to various staff.

Be aware of your child's location when you visit in homes.
People of all cultures love children, but they may not demonstrate
it in appropriate ways. Someone may want to pick up your child
and carry her off to show everyone around the neighborhood. To
be suddenly grabbed and taken off by a stranger can be frightening to a child as well as dangerous. Offer the opportunity for relationship and friendship with your child in your presence and be
willing to say "no" when it is appropriate.

Dispel false assumptions about your character. Often men in
Islamic cultures assume they can be more "familiar" and intrusive
in relating to Western women as compared with women of their
own culture. Find ways to communicate to your neighbors that
you are not like the foreigners they see on television. When our
family first moved into our neighborhood overseas, people were
curious to see if we were like those they saw on CNN. When we
dressed in local styles and acted conservatively, our neighbors
treated us with respect.

**Teach your children culturally-appropriate relational
boundaries.** In the country where I grew up, friendship was
demonstrated by hand holding with someone of the same gender. However it was considered totally inappropriate for a man to
hold hands with or touch a woman other than his wife. There
were differences in "personal space," eye contact and posture. Talk
through these differences with your daughter. Help her to recognize when the neighbor's son is taking inappropriate liberties by
sitting next to her on the sofa or shaking her hand.

**Make sure your home environment promotes openness
and communication.** As your daughter grows, talk about the
issues that affect her. Tell her why you have chosen to raise her in
an Islamic country and explain what "incarnational ministry"
means. Specify the ways in which you have chosen to identify
with the local culture and the ways in which you have chosen to
be different. Your daughter needs to understand some of the rea-
soning behind decisions that affect her. She may have a lot of

questions and comments. Let her communicate her feelings honestly. Over-spiritualizing difficulties or valiantly trying only to focus on the positive, will make her feel as though she isn't being heard. Affirm that, yes, there are some difficult aspects of living here. Ask her, "What are the things that are the hardest for you right now? What resources might God provide for dealing with them?" Involve your daughter in the process of making lifestyle decisions, letting her know you value her input.

Recognize the signs and symptoms of sexual abuse.

I received an email from a woman serving in an Islamic country. She wrote: "For me, the thought of [sexual abuse] happening to my precious little girl was so horrendous that even though I suspected it subconsciously, my conscious mind would never allow it to come to the surface. So my daughter's abuse went on for months before I finally could not ignore it any longer, and reality came crashing in. Praise God she reacted violently to the abuse with nightmares and terror, or who knows if I ever would have known."

Knowing some of the possible signs of abuse can lead to early intervention. Here are some of them: nightmares, terror of the dark or other sleep disturbances, unusual fear of strangers or of specific individuals known to the family, unusual fear of separation from parents or of being left with a babysitter, physical bruising or abrasions, vaginal infections or inflammation, loss of appetite, behavioral problems, depression or withdrawal, loss of interest in normal activities and involvements, and unusual mood swings or weepiness.

If abuse does occur, it needs to be dealt with immediately at two levels: first with the victim and then, with the abuser. The victim needs to know that it is safe to talk, that no topic is off-limits, and that she will be heard lovingly and without accusation. She needs to see you act as her advocate, showing just anger in her defense against the perpetrator. Seeing your reaction of concern and anger communicates that you believe what happened was a violation against her and is a key ingredient to a good recovery.

Cloaking the incident in secrecy confuses the child. She may feel that she was the one who did wrong instead of the abuser. She may believe that she somehow deserved what happened. She may feel you are ashamed of her. Statistics indicate that sexually abused children more frequently enter abusive relationships later in life. Some of this may be related to the secrecy and mixed signals they receive at the time of the event.

If the incident of abuse is very traumatic, it is wise to get help from a quali-
fied counselor. Some studies have shown that a person who is effectively
debriefed within 24 to 72 hours after a traumatic event is less likely to experience long-term effects such as depression or Post Traumatic Stress Disorder.
Prompt, appropriate intervention can make a big difference in recovery.

The perpetrator of the abuse also needs to be dealt with immediately, in a just
and godly manner. This can be a real dilemma on the mission field. We are so
geared towards being sensitive to the culture, that our response can place a
higher value on being tactful rather than biblical. Sometimes we want to "gently correct," rather than confront someone directly with the truth and apply just
consequences to wrong actions.

If the abuser is not clearly confronted, the message communicated to the
child is that God's program for the unsaved is more important than his care for
his children. Missionaries need to know that incarnational ministry includes
Jesus' uncompromising hatred of sin. In clearly evil situations, there is freedom
to confront and oppose evil, even if it goes against what is considered to be culturally correct. This does not exclude prayer, forgiveness and the possibility of
reconciliation and restoration; hopefully all of that can happen. But even in the
instance of repentance and restoration, the perpetrator should be removed
from ongoing contact with the child.

One last point on this topic. Both sexual abuse or harassment and the signs
of that abuse can be very subtle. The absence of signs of abuse doesn't neces-
sarily prove the absence of abuse. Whether or not symptoms occur, parents
need to be aware, cautious, and in good communication with their children.

Must life within the borders of Islam be lived in fear and defensiveness? No.
It is possible to live in an Islamic culture with confidence and joy. However, it
is also possible to quietly build into our lifestyles wise safeguards and guidelines that flow from a truthful assessment of our surroundings. An important
ingredient in raising radiant daughters in dark places is protecting them from
preventable harm.

God's truth modeled in positive, intimate relationships

A friend recently shared what she thought was the single most important
positive influence in raising a daughter in an Islamic context: a strong marriage
relationship between her parents. The home is where a girl deeply and personally experiences the truth. Think for a moment of the negative input your

daughter is receiving from Islam. What does she need to see and experience when she walks through the front door of her own home? She needs a powerful reconfirmation of biblical truth.

As she watches how her father relates to her mother, she will notice every nuance of conversation, courtesy and caring. She will be evaluating whether the truths that are spoken match those that are lived. When "spoken truth" resonates with "lived-out truth," it becomes "integrated truth." It is finally accepted as truly true! What truths are being confirmed to your daughter through your marriage?

Almost as important as the relationship between a husband and wife, is the one between a father and his daughter. How he relates to her sends strong signals about her value. When he expresses his dreams for her and encourages her to excel, it gives her hope that she does, in fact, have potential. When a father makes time and expresses physical affection, he communicates much more than just, "I love you." His actions say, "I enjoy you. I like spending time with you."

Some of my favorite childhood memories are of times spent with my Dad—yearly camping and fishing trips, stories heard and songs sung from the safety of his lap. A father is the closest male relationship a girl knows. He models God to her. If he is distant and uninvolved, she begins to believe that God is that way too. She learns that she isn't worth God's time and attention. Her innate sense of value is diminished and, instead of verifying the Truth to her, the preoccupied father reconfirms the lies told by the culture.

A mother's role is also vital. She's the one who must take the initiative in helping her daughter find friends, learn cultural cues and discover the parameters of her new world. Think carefully about the picture of womanhood you model to your daughter. Does it show strength, dignity, joy, and gentleness of spirit? Does it demonstrate your God-given intellect, ability and spiritual gifts? When I think of my own mother, I think of someone who welled up with humor in the most disgruntling of situations. I think of her openhearted hospitality and her hopes for the national girls she encouraged and educated.

A daughter absorbs attitudes toward the culture largely from her mother. It is so easy in an Islamic environment for women to develop a sense of defeat, frustration and hopelessness. A little girl can hear a lot about what she can't do, instead of positive messages about what she can do. What types of ministry can your daughter be involved in? Becoming active in caring for others goes a long way in offsetting a negative, defeated, and complaining spirit. A girl can learn resilience, joy and spiritual stability from her mother. She can learn that radiant living isn't primarily dictated by external circumstances but by the internal condition of the heart.

Other people in the community can model truth to your daughter as well. I think of the boarding staff and teachers at the school I attended for twelve years. I think of those in particular who were consistent "truth-tellers" as they lived out the faith they professed. "Auntie Eva" was a twice-retired missionary in her seventies who returned to our school to help. Her beautiful, nut-brown hair fell to her knees and she washed it with laundry detergent. Auntie Eva knew the names of a thousand birds and flowers and was perpetually awestruck at God's creative genius. Each child in the school was known by name and prayed for daily on her knees. She chose a verse for each graduating senior and prayed us through the transition to college. She was quick to laugh, to admonish and to encourage. She liked us children and we knew it. She made me think that maybe Jesus liked me too.

We talk often about living in community and being the body of Christ. How committed are we to each other's children on the field? Do we ignore them or treat them as though they are invisible? Or do we encourage, nurture and enjoy them as significant members of that body?

The truth about our daughters

One of the joys of nurturing our children is witnessing the gradual unfolding of the unique design God had in mind when He carefully formed them. As you raise your daughter, watch for the special ingredients God blended together to form her identity. Some of these ingredients include the shaping of her multicultural environment, her personality and abilities and her femininity. Your careful nurturing of these key areas of identity will go a long way in offsetting negative input. Let's look at these identity issues a little more closely.

Her multicultural environment

As a child I learned some of my most important life skills from "Ummi." She was the wife of our cook, and I called her the local name for Mommy. She taught me how to launder clothes with a bar of soap and a stick. She taught me how to build a fire and grind spices with a mortar and pestle. She taught me lullabies that still sing me to sleep.

As the child of a missionary, your daughter is a multicultural person. She needs your encouragement to fully enjoy this aspect of her being. Sometimes as parents we can feel uneasy when our children bond deeply with the local culture. There's a twinge of regret when they prefer chicken curry and mangoes to steak and apple pie. In some ways we want our children to be just like us—to feel the same connections with our roots that we do. We want their "home" to be our "home" so that throughout life our families will always migrate back to the same place together. Your daughter needs you to take the risk of allowing her to fully enjoy her multicultural personality. It's part of God's special design for her, and the closer she comes to deeply enjoying that design, the happier she will be.

Help your daughter to explore some of the things local women and girls enjoy. Have fun with their styles of dress. Find out what's in fashion, go clothes shopping, and design outfits together. Paint toenails. Experiment with hairstyles. Wear bracelets and nose rings! Draw some of the women and girls in the neighborhood into your learning experience. Use it as a time to encourage deep friendships with girls who are members of the culture.

The other side of the multicultural balancing act, however, is the identity-links your daughter feels to your "home" culture. She isn't, in fact, a member of the local culture, and she needs to be raised in a way that affirms her national identity. This is especially difficult to do when you are trying to be sensitive to the Islamic values and expectations around you. You don't want to offend, but at the same time you may want to allow your daughter more freedom than local women have.

On furlough your daughter will experience a host of outlets she may never have known on the field. It could be hard for her to return to the Islamic environment and suddenly feel suffocated by dress codes and lifestyle restrictions. How can you make these transitions easier for her to bear and still affirm the identity-links she feels with her "home" country?

We need to be especially sensitive to not push "incarnational living" further than our daughters can bear. As a family, we used to specifically build "culture breaks" into our lifestyle. My daughter and I had a ladies' day out once a month when we would dress in Western-style clothing and go to a fancy hotel for lunch. Another outlet was membership in the athletic facilities of the international school in our city. Within the walls of that campus our daughter could wear shorts, do tae kwon do, play T-ball, swim or take ballet lessons. Sometimes we planned a family weekend at a Western-style hotel.

Culture breaks can also happen inside your own home. Our last home overseas had an upstairs section with three bedrooms and a family room. Downstairs we had a guestroom, office, and living area where hospitality happened day and night. But no one was allowed upstairs except family and close friends who were invited. I limited the times of day when our house-helper was allowed there. Our family could have our own time together to read stories, watch videos and play games. Our daughter could wear shorts, do aerobics, dance and sing. It was our private family space.

Culture breaks can also happen through various schooling options. As a girl growing up in an Islamic culture, I was thankful to be sent to a boarding school where, within the parameters of the school, I had the freedom to act and dress more like a Westerner. When my husband and I returned overseas, we had the opportunity to send our children to an international school offering numerous creative outlets and extracurricular activities. I've heard of very successful home-schooling groups that meet regularly, have field trips, and organize activities that might not otherwise be possible. Think of outlets and activities to expand your daughter's horizons.

Her unique personality and feminine identity

I remember as a small child learning the little things that made me different from every other person. Not many of my friends nourished their hearts with the rhythms of poetry. No one else could perch in the branches of a tree, listen to the wind and think the thoughts I was thinking. Not many loved to spend time alone in the woods collecting flowers and ferns and making elf houses with bits of bark and moss. No one else made stories the way I made them.

One of the most wonderful gifts you can give your daughter is affirmation of her identity. What are the things that are unique to her alone? What is she able to do that no one else can do quite so well? What feeds her soul? What makes her eyes sparkle and laugh? How can you encourage and nourish all the wonderful and various aspects of her being, her personal relationship with God, her intellect, her femininity, her physical body and her relational skills?

In an Islamic context, it can be so easy for girls to end up with squashed and defeated personalities. Don't let it happen! Be intentional in the way you nurture your daughter. This is especially important in the area of her feminine identity. Tell her why it is so special to be a woman. Give her biographies to read of strong, believing women who overcame great obstacles: Corrie ten Boom, Elisabeth Elliot, Amy Carmichael, Lilias Trotter, Maya Angelou and Mother Theresa. Encourage her to stretch her mind.

Give her the life skills and experiences she needs to develop confidence and competence. Involve her in decision-making, teaching her how to make choices and take responsibility. Assign tasks. Ask for her opinion. As she gets older, teach her some practical life-skills: how to manage finances, how to drive, how to schedule appointments for herself, how to find a job, how to use a computer. Some of these can be hard to do in an Islamic context and may require some creative thinking.

Most importantly, teach your daughter a biblical view of womanhood. She needs to know deeply, at a feeling level, what it means to be created in the "image of God." Teach her that God thinks she is of such value that he died to redeem her. Introduce her to women of the Bible who played key roles in redemptive history.

Hagar was the mother of the line of Ishmael. She was an Egyptian woman, a slave-girl, a nobody. Yet God loved her so much that he pursued her far into the desert and tenderly cared for her. Hagar gave God a name. She said, "You are the God who sees me" (Gen 16:13). Maybe that's the name our daughters should carry with them as they grow up in regions where the daughters of Ishmael dwell … where there are veils and walls. They need to know that, even in those stony, desert places, they are seen by God—a God who is able to make springs of sweet waters to satisfy their hearts. They need to know the joy of lifting their eyes to his face and responding with Hagar, "I have now seen the one who sees me." Psalm 34:5 says, "Those who look to him are radiant, their faces are never covered with shame." What a joy to see the reflected radiance of God in the faces of our daughters!

Adapted from the article originally published by Interact, a publication for MK care and education.

For copies of the original article or reprint information, please contact Interact, P.O. Box 863, Wheaton, ILL 60189 or contact Janet Blomberg using e-mail, janetblomberg@compuserve.com.

Emily Van Dalen grew up in an Islamic country. She and her husband served overseas as missionaries for twelve years with the Associate Reformed Presbyterians and continue with them as home-based missionaries. She is personally involved with Cedar Springs, based in Columbia, SC which ministers to missionaries and their families.

PART TWO

Ministry to Muslim Women

Open Hearts
Open Homes

by Doreen Corley

Having been born and raised in Illinois among cornfields and soybeans, I never suspected all that God had in mind for my life. I've been married for 50 years to my wonderful husband, Dick. We have four grown children, all of whom are married and living for the Lord. Each couple has given us two grandchildren, so you can see how wealthy we are.

We served with Christar beginning in 1955. We spent twenty-five years in Iran, one in the Philippines, five in the home office, and eight in Turkey.

I grew up in a home where hospitality wasn't practiced very much. After Dick and I were married and he was struggling to finish his education, we didn't practice hospitality much either. I am sure some of you can relate to that situation.

Little did we know then that God would send us to a country where hospitality is practiced all of the time: it was expected that I would love people and want to be with them, either in my home or theirs. To them, being alone was a deplorable state to be remedied as quickly as possible! Thus, it became clear to me early on that I must learn how to have an open heart and an open home. It doesn't come naturally. We like our privacy. People who know me now say, "That's just how you are, relaxed and hospitable." Not so, for it is something I have learned; and now I love it.

"Open heart—open home" is an attitude of the heart. We go to other lands because we want to follow God and do what his Word says. First then, let's see what the Bible says about being hospitable. Hebrews 13:2, 3 says we are to entertain strangers. 1 Timothy 3:2 says we are to be "given to hospitality." I take that to mean we are to use our energy, time and resources in pursuit of it. 1 Peter 4:9 reminds us to be hospitable without complaining—and no under-the-breath murmuring! Since the Bible is a Middle-Eastern book, it is replete with examples of hospitality: Abraham and three strangers (who turned out to be angels), the Philippian jailer who took in Paul and Silas, and, in Acts, the people Paul and his ship's crew stayed with for three days.

Let's explore a bit further why hospitality plays an important role in our ministries to Muslims:

- Welcoming friends into our homes nurtures closer relationships. There's something special about breaking bread together; it somehow binds us to one another.
- Graciously caring for our friends breaks down prejudice. Muslims have much prejudice toward Christians; we have the same toward Muslims.
- Hospitality leads to repeated contact, for your guests will invite you back to their home. After they learn to trust you, they will share their hearts more openly.
- A home atmosphere will relax your Muslim friends. They will see a Christian "up close," maybe for the first time. Questions will arise in their minds, and they will voice these.
- Hospitality enables your friends to feel comfortable in a peaceful home, even though they know you are a Christian.
- Having an open home gives opportunity for you to show a film, like the JESUS film. You may be able to give them some literature or a good book.

How do you begin a ministry of hospitality? It begins in your heart, your open heart—a heart that loves others and wants to reach out to them. Have you ever been in a home where you have felt unwanted and in the way? That is such an uncomfortable situation in which to be. Please make sure your heart is open and ready to receive friends. Guests are "dear ones from God"—special ones. Make them feel that way.

First, you must develop friendships, and that takes time. Ask questions, but not the threatening kind. Muslim people may ask many personal questions; for example, "How much did you pay for this rug?" or "How much salary do you get, and who pays it?" Get used to these and have answers for them.

Bond with your new friends. Share pictures of your family. Your visitors will want you to come to their home so they can reciprocate with their family photos. Speak kindly to your friends and show them consideration.

Hospitality can be shown anytime your doorbell rings, if you tune your heart that way. Always serve something. Put the tea water on as you pass to answer the door. I had a special spot in my living room for candy, cookies and nuts, small serving plates and a box of Kleenex (used for napkins where I served). I was ready!

Greet your guests in the same manner they greet one another, be it with a hug or a kiss on the cheek or both. Tell them how happy you are to see them. If you invite them, make sure you serve their ethnic food. Iranians don't know what to do with mashed potatoes! Your friends will enjoy their own kind of food and will appreciate it even more when you learn to cook it their way. Ask someone to teach you. Rice and chicken is always a good choice.

When you are invited to a friend's home, take a small gift like candy, flowers or fruit. Be sure to take off your shoes, especially if you see a pile of footwear at the door. Look around the room and find a seat near the door. Don't take the "upper seat" as that is reserved for favored guests. Relax and enjoy the time with them.

Plan to have guests on a regular basis. We chose one night a week and invited folks to come. We invited people on Thursday evening, which is like our Saturday evening here. This takes discipline, but it is worth the effort it requires. Pray before the meal, and say, "It's our custom to thank God for the food." In your own home you can do what you like, so take advantage of this. We often pray with our guests just before they leave, especially concerning some problem we have discussed during the evening. Yes, we do this with Muslim people and they appreciate it very much. We do ask permission to pray for them but have never been refused.

While in Chicago, Dick met Hamid, an Iranian fellow at a college. He invited Hamid to come for an Iranian meal with us. He came with his Catholic girl-friend and a bottle of wine as a gift. From then on he was at our house two or three times each week. We ate together, talked together and after nine months he was saved and has been serving the Lord fervently since. He has led Bible studies and many Iranians have come to know the Lord. Hospitality has paid off in duplicating and multiplying our ministry.

One cold night in Istanbul, we got off a bus and heard a couple talking Farsi. We chatted for a few minutes and invited them to come for tea. Dick jotted our phone number on the back of a tract, and we waited several weeks before they called and wanted to come. The story is glorious. We drank tea, ate cookies, munched sunflower seeds and talked. She wanted to know more, so Dick gave her a Farsi New Testament. She went on to Denmark, but her fiance' smuggled himself to Greece and was put in jail. The only thing he had to read was the Farsi New Testament, and he found the Lord. Back in Denmark the girl also was saved! They got together, got married and went to Bible school. Her mother came from Iran, received Jesus and returned to Iran where her son and daughter-in-law also were saved. Finally her drunken husband also became a believer. Where did it all start? It started by inviting the young couple in for tea and cookies!

Below are questions to consider about the ministry of hospitality:

1. What are some hindrances you face in hospitality?
2. Why are some families reluctant to have people in their homes?
3. What precautions should be taken in hospitality?
4. What is the difference between hospitality and entertaining?
5. Why are Westerners not having guests regularly? Is it money, space, or time?
6. Did you grow up in a home where you had many guests? If yes, describe it.
7. Is your pastor hospitable? In what ways?

Doreen Corley worked in the Middle East for twenty-five years. She has been involved in working with orphans, teaching nationals, boarding missionary kids and visitation. She has also done church planting among refugees.

Mentoring and Building Community among Women Muslim Background Believers: A Case Study

by P. R.

A few years ago, I looked around at the group of North African Christians (Muslim Background Believers or MBBs) in our French city, and I suddenly realized that there had been some changes. What had been a group of mostly single students was a now a group with many young married women, some with young children. I knew that when I got married, in spite of premarital counseling and plenty of books, I didn't have any idea what marriage was all about; I figured that these ladies were in the same situation. I also noticed that these women were isolated from each other. Many of the MBBs attended French churches and met with one another monthly for fellowship and evangelism. While the women enjoyed being together once a month, they were reticent to initiate deeper relationships. So I decided to start a women's group.

The group was based on the idea in Titus 2, that the older women teach the younger women; it focused on marriage and later, as more children arrived, child-rearing and family issues. Some on our team questioned the need for such a group. One person told me that because Arabs don't have the same expectations in marriage as Westerners, they don't have as many conflicts. Others asked what in the world I would teach these women. I replied that I would teach them things I wished I had known in the beginning of my marriage and that I would also try to teach them to avoid the mistakes that I had made. Since I had made plenty of mistakes, I had no lack of material!

So, with very little confidence in myself, but with a vision and a burden for these women, I started the group. We studied and laughed and cried and prayed through those first years of marriage, dealing with topics such as communication, forgiveness, in-laws, money and the all-time favorite topic of sex. Special attention was given to relate these topics to the women's North African culture.

During the first two years, we only met monthly as the women had studies, jobs or other responsibilities. Then, as the babies arrived, the need for more support increased. Young mothers can often feel isolated, so we started meeting weekly to discuss child-rearing. The women greatly appreciated the teaching and grew both in their confidence as mothers and in godliness as women and wives. I always made it clear to them that I was teaching them as the older woman in Titus 2, so that one day they would be the older women, the mentors who teach others; and they are currently doing just that.

Modeling service

While our relationships deepened through time, the road to building a serving, loving community was a bit more of a challenge. The first time one of the women had a baby after we started the group, I tried to organize meals for her. No one could find the time to help. Once, we gave a party for a woman who had adopted a baby. Everyone was supposed to bring something. One person brought a cake, but others just brought a little box of juice or a small package of cookies. I had to empty my cupboards to supply the abundance of food required to honor our guest of honor. However, little by little, as the women experienced the blessing of being served—having meals brought to them when babies were born, being visited in sickness and grief or attending parties given—they soon recognized the blessing of serving and began to do this for each other. It was modeling and encouraging that taught this idea of community.

Now, all these things happen spontaneously between the women. When a special evangelist was coming, we wanted to have a meal after the meeting. At the time I was preparing for furlough and was exhausted. I said to the women, "I'm tired, and I can't do this. You're capable of doing this. I'll guide you through it, but you do it." So, we discussed an affordable menu, assigned tasks, and chose a coordinator.

The evening went beautifully; they were so pleased, and so was I. The woman who coordinated the evening said to me, "I never thought that I was useful to God, but you showed me that God could use even me." This woman hasn't stopped serving the Lord ever since. Before my furlough, the women organized a going away party for me and for a colleague who was retiring, complete with an abundance of food, dancing and great entertainment. They did a beautiful job, and I was very touched.

Mentoring

Having described our women's group, how it got started and how it functioned, I now want to look at some of the underlying principles that provide the foundation for such a group. The two basic principles are mentoring (Titus 2) and building community. Mentoring is the principle expressed in Titus 2, that the older women are to teach the younger. A lot is being written on this subject today, so I won't go into the reasons or the need for it. We'll just accept that mentoring is good and necessary and that the Bible says we should do it.

If there is a need for mentoring in general, the need is even more acute for MBBs. As one woman expressed, "We grew up in North African Muslim homes with one set of values and teaching; we've grown up in France with another set of values and teaching, and now we're Christians. We need to evaluate everything in our past, our culture and our education in light of the Bible and decide what is good and can be kept and what needs to change. What you're doing here, teaching us and helping us to relate the Bible to our culture and past is invaluable. You're helping us to make a new way, a North African Christian way to live and think."

Even Muslim women are eager for mentors. How many of my young neighbors try to emulate my life, even down to my decorating style! I tell them that there is no power to live my life outside of Jesus, but they still try to put the varnish of Christian values and behavior on their Muslim lives. Perhaps one day the truth will penetrate. All women are in need of mentors, and we shouldn't be timid in proposing this type of relationship. I must admit that I started our women's group in fear and trembling, my voice and hands literally shaking as I spoke in what seemed to me very faltering French. In spite of that, the women responded to the way I honestly dealt with issues that touched their lives as I shared my own struggles and the sufficiency of God's Word and his Holy Spirit to change us. So, I think we can and should have much confidence in pursuing mentoring relationships with women.

Pitfalls to avoid

That said, there are some dangers to be avoided in mentoring relationships. One danger is to appear as if you have no struggles. It's what I call the "be perfect as I am perfect" image. This makes you unapproachable, and it discourages the women who think they can never attain the same level of spirituality as you. If you openly share the struggles you faced in getting to where you are and the struggles you face today, they will have hope. Together you will repent and pray for God's grace in your lives. You, too, will see that there is not a lot of difference between you and them. We are all in immense need of God's forgiveness and grace.

Many times I have been talking with someone about an issue, for example, not returning evil for evil in a marriage; they listen as I explain, but their eyes light up when I give an example of when I've said things or wanted to say things just to hurt my husband after he had hurt me. That's when they really start to listen. It's as if they think, "You know my life. You know what I experience. I can trust what you say." Transparency is an essential element in a mentoring ministry.

Creating dependency is another danger in mentoring relationships. Too often, the missionary or mentor becomes the hub of a wheel. Each woman in the group has a strong relationship with the mentor but a much weaker relationship with other group members; when the mentor leaves, the group falls apart. We need to weave a cloth of interdependent relationships among women. This needs to be intentional on the part of the mentor: building community among those in the group, teaching them to care for each other rather than relying on her for all their support and needs.

In our group, if someone was in need, I'd encourage the women to call her or visit her during the week. I generally let the women initiate contact with me outside the meeting. They contacted me when they needed me. Sometimes it was serious—counseling, rescuing (we had two cases of battered women), comforting in sickness or death. Sometimes it was light—meals or outings together, chatting on the phone or taking the kids to the pool. I was available to them. They were and are my friends, but I continually encouraged the women to minister to one another.

Another danger related to dependency is failure to transfer leadership and responsibility to the women. In this case the women look to the mentor to do all the ministry and don't feel capable themselves. Again, the mentor has to intentionally communicate her objective from the beginning. I always told the women, "I am teaching you for the moment so that you, in your turn, will be the older women who teach others. You will not always need me to teach you." I also intentionally pointed out to them what I saw as their spiritual gifts and how

I saw God using them to minister to others.

Opportunities to minister together, for instance, putting on dinners and parties and preparing meals for the sick, helped them to grow in the confidence that God had gifted them and could use them. Many of these women now have dynamic evangelistic ministries among other women in their neighborhoods. Two took the initiative to begin Bible studies with a new believer who wanted to be baptized. One discipled her sister, who then in turn, discipled a friend. Another has a heart for bringing people together into supportive, loving Christian community. In addition, they minister to the practical needs of the saints with meals, housecleaning, visits and childcare. I have a lot of admiration for these women.

Sometimes the issue of a missionary's motives comes up in mentoring relationships when dealing with transferring leadership and responsibility for ministry. We missionaries will say that our goal is to train believers for ministry; but when it comes down to it, we are reluctant to give up control. A coach for church planters once said that he had never seen a situation in which the church planters turned over the work too soon. He said that, generally, the missionary thinks the believers aren't ready and that often the believers themselves are timid about taking responsibility, content to let the missionaries do it. The result is a happy little co-dependent relationship.

Thus, we need to continually evaluate our own motivations in ministry. Are we deriving our identity from our work? Is that identity threatened by giving control of the work to the believers? If we find our identity, our purpose, our sense of self-worth in being the missionary—the professional who does the ministry and teaching—then training others to take over what we do will threaten us. We won't have the patience to let them learn and fail and progress, because we can already do it so much better, and that's our job, right? Instead, in our mentoring, we need to keep before us the goal of training others, enabling them for ministry and turning leadership over to them. We also need to have our identity firmly rooted not in what we do, but in who we are in Christ. We need to be constantly evaluating our motives and rooting out the idols that take hold of our hearts: personal glory, reputation, self-worth, and control.

Focusing on character

The key to effective mentoring or discipleship among MBBs is addressing Christian character. To feed believers abstract theology or vague biblical teaching without precise application is to neglect the areas of Christian character and obedience. We place a lot of emphasis on family relationships. We tell people that they can have great ministries, but if they can't love their spouses and kids, their ministries are not worth much. It's in the home that we see the extent of our sanctification and progress in the Christian life.

We develop with people a theology with practical implications. For instance, we develop a theology of suffering along with applications of not returning evil for evil and not taking vengeance into our own hands. We develop a theology of sex, helping people to think biblically about sex so that their thoughts, behavior, and how they teach their children are affected. It is important, we see once again, to be transparent and to share our own work in applying the Bible to our lives and character, especially when it's difficult and will cost something.

Mentoring and discipleship also need to address a person's culture. Discipleship and teaching must go deeper than just teaching the Bible. We must identify cultural practices and values, evaluate them in light of the Bible and decide how behavior needs to change. If our discipleship is simply teaching the Bible without helping people to see how both their past and their culture affect their behavior, then change will be just superficial.

Take, for example, child-rearing. In North African culture, boys are generally spoiled and allowed to do what they want; girls are closely controlled; and lying is an acceptable method for controlling children. These are often unconscious behaviors and values. So, if we just teach broadly what the Bible says about children without discussing the practices and values of the culture, those values and habits will never be examined in the light of Scripture. However, we need to carefully evaluate whether what we are teaching is biblical or simply a reflection of our own cultural values. A fixed bedtime for children might be helpful, but it is not a biblical mandate.

Another example that was important in our women's group and remains relevant to Christian and Muslim couples alike: the area of marriage. We're all sinners, and marriage is difficult because it involves two selfish sinners trying to live together. It's not that one culture has more or less problems in marriage; rather, each has a different twist on the same problems. In-law problems are often more pronounced in North African culture because couples often live with or are financially tied to the family. North African culture fosters competition between the mother-in-law and daughter-in-law for the son/husband's love and attention. A son is his mother's retirement plan. It is in a mother-in-law's best interest to keep him attached to her and not to his wife.

Genesis is a good place to see God's plan for marriage and family relationships. A man leaving his father and mother and cleaving to his wife represents the one flesh and the intimacy of marriage. How that works itself out will be different in each culture. For a Muslim man, this probably does not mean walking down the street hand in hand with his wife or to giving up his male friends and confiding everything in his bride. But the Bible is clear that one of the reasons for marriage is intimacy and, if that's totally lacking, there's something wrong with the marriage, no matter what the culture says.

As I talk to women, read Arab women's magazines (non-Christian ones) and listen to popular music, I find that North African women have many of the same desires as Western women. They want tenderness, love, appreciation, and communication, a real relationship with their husband. They might not express these desires in the same way as those in the West, but if a wife wants this, the husband needs to find ways to meet these desires in a culturally appropriate way. Of course, I work with the women, so my message to them is that they can't change their husbands; they can change only themselves. They need to pray for their husbands and work on repenting and changing their own worldly ways of control and vengeance: critical spirits, manipulation and withholding sex. They need to trust God to change their husbands and ask God to work change in themselves.

Building community

Together with mentoring, building community was the other foundational goal of the women's group. The women remain isolated from one another for several reasons. One that I struggled with was fear and a lack of confidence—fear that if I approach someone, I might be bothering them; they won't have the time or they won't want to spend time with me. The fact is that we almost all have these feelings, and it takes just one person to break through the isolation and begin to connect with others. Another reason for isolation is busyness. Everyone is busy and thinks of others as being too busy to connect. Even women in more traditional North African communities are beginning to work outside the home. What's more is that immigrant populations are becoming increasingly dispersed, and traditional support structures are being lost.

Isolation is sometimes bred by mistrust and suspicion. I found that this was not an issue among the women in our group who had grown up in France as second generation immigrants. However, among my Muslim neighbors and the first generation MBBs, it is a big issue. Mistrust and suspicion are present in most relationships outside the family unit. I know so many women who are lonely because they don't trust anyone. "You start to get to know people, and you only have problems," they say. They trust me, however. They know I won't gossip about them. But I can't be every lonely Muslim woman's best friend. Even among the believers of the first generation, I often have to point out their suspicion of other believers and direct them to 1 Corinthians 13: "Love hopes all things and believes all things." This mistrust can destroy a group and must be dealt with.

Building trust takes time. Mentors need to be transparent. Sharing openly shows our trust and encourages the women to follow suit. I stressed in the group that everything shared among us was to stay among us and was not to be shared with others. The integrity of trust must be guarded from the destructive power of gossip. Another element in building trust was simply spending time together getting to know one another. In our group, relationships were built as each woman took turns hosting us at her home. This social aspect is very important in building trust and community.

Another aspect of building community is learning to serve each other and to serve together. We work toward becoming a loving, serving community. I found that these women had lost some of the habits that their first generation immigrant mothers have: visiting the sick, taking meals to people, doing housework for someone in need, listening and counseling. They had become very Western in this way, each one taking care of her own needs alone. In fact, some of these women say that I gave them back their culture: things they had rejected as old-fashioned or had just lost, they've regained. They have discovered a pride in the positive aspects of their culture.

I described in the beginning of this article our first, faltering efforts in learning to serve. It was by modeling, encouraging, and experiencing the benefits of being served that the women began to serve in practical ways. It was a conscious effort to include everyone in service and not just to do it all myself. Over time, trust was built, relationships deepened, and practical service became a natural response, as did spiritual ministry to one another.

I see a great need for effective mentoring that addresses Christian character and obedience and that engages a person's culture biblically. Efforts should be made to be transparent in our teaching and modeling, to foster relationships between the women, and to train them for ministry. Priority should be given to building community by bringing people together, creating an environment of trust and learning to serve each other and to serve together.

P.R. has worked among North African immigrants in Europe since 1980.

Chronological Bible Storying
by Annette Hall

Chronological Bible Storying (CBS) is a method of evangelization that allows us to reach individuals and groups who prefer oral communication. It began developing as a method in the 1970s in Southeast Asia and the Islands. CBS has evolved from chronological teaching to chronological story telling to "storying" the Bible. Storying is the intentional use of Bible narratives as the primary teaching tool, along with appropriate guided discussion. Today, across the world, we are storying the Bible chronologically to oral communicators. With the use of CBS, we can evangelize, disciple, plant churches and train leaders among oral communicators who have never learned to read a word.

Before explaining CBS in detail, I need to explain who oral communicators are. Oral communicators are individuals who prefer to get their information through oral rather than literate means. There are three levels of oral communicators. These levels are shown on the learning grid which appears on the next page.

The *total illiterate* has never been to school. She can neither write her name nor recognize written words. She may not even know how to read a picture properly. She receives and processes all her information through oral means. She is good at memorizing recipes, directions, and stories. While she may sit and listen politely to a series of points or lists of important facts, she cannot apply them to her situation. Instead she learns through stories rather than facts. Stories help her process information by finding parallels to her own situation and then applying these parallels to her life. In order to anchor the truths, see how these truths relate to life, and retain the stories through memorization, she needs to hear the stories in chronological order.

Here is an example of how this process works. I told the story of Abraham, Sarah, Hagar and Ishmael to a group of illiterate women. When I finished the

"How People Learn and the use of Exposition A Learning Grid" Chart

Oral Communication / Illiterate	Oral Communication / Functional Illiterate	Oral Communication / Semi-Illiterate	Oral/Literate Communication / Literate	Literate Communication / Highly Literate
STORY				
No Exposition	No Exposition	Some Exposition	Story with Exposition / or Exposition	As Much Exposition as Desired / or Interest Calls For
EXPOSITION				
DIALOGUE				
No Exposition	Little Exposition	Moderate Exposition	Exposition in Dialogue	As Much Exposition as Desired / or Interest Calls For

Used by permission of Jim Slack

story, one woman spoke up and said, "That's a true story. God gave Abraham and Sarah a promise. They didn't have the faith to wait on the promise but acted on their own. Look at all the trouble that came to them. It happens all the time. God promises something and people won't wit for God to do his promise." She said all this without any teaching or prompting from the group.

The *functionally illiterate* woman has been to school and can write her name. However, she has completed only a few months or years of education and since leaving school she has not continued to read. She has lost the ability to gain information through the written word. She never picks up a book, newspaper or magazine to read for pleasure. While her government would consider her literate, she gathers all her information orally. Since she has been to school, she can process small amounts of teaching, but long lectures or lists may escape her. She prefers to hear a story, process the information contained in the story, and apply it to her life.

The *semi-literate* has gone further in school. She can read when necessary and may even have a job that requires some ability to read. She does not read for pleasure, but gathers all her information orally. She can follow information given through a lecture format but, given a choice, she will listen to a story. She is able to memorize lists of facts and reproduce them, but she has difficulty in applying those lists to life situations. She can't easily analyze and choose from the list in order to make her decisions. Because she has been to school, she can handle more teaching during the story session and during the dialogue session. She probably doesn't need as many stories to learn a biblical truth as does the woman who is totally illiterate. Most Muslim women fall into one of these three levels of oral competency.

Most missionary women fall into the last two categories of literate and highly literate learners shown on the learning grid. These women have lost the ability to use oral communication. Using myself as an example, I need to use a recipe nearly every time I cook. I have friends who cook wonderful meals and never look at a recipe. If I watch a friend cook couscous, I need to write down what she does so that I can reproduce it at home. My friend comes to visit me and watches me bake a cake and then goes home to make the same cake without written instructions. I have difficulty memorizing my own telephone number. My friend has the numbers of all her friends memorized. I have lost the ability to memorize easily what I see and hear. To get to a new place, I check the map and then write down the directions: go two circles and turn left; go to the sixth street and turn right. My natural tendency is to find someone who uses my preferred communication style. To evangelize the majority of Muslim women, I must change my style to their preferred learning style. To evangelize, I am the one who must adapt and change rather than expecting them to do so. Therefore, I have had to retrain myself to memorize and tell stories.

The learning grid lists the five levels of literacy as explained above. In addition, the learning grid divides a story or learning session into two parts. The top half—or the story part—is when the story is told or read. The bottom half is when the discussion takes place. For the totally illiterate, no teaching takes place. Rather, all learning comes from the story. I tell the story. I ask the women to repeat the story. I ask questions about what the characters in the story did. I ask what the story means to them. I don't teach.

I have memorized the learning grid. I try to place every woman I meet on the grid. Once I have determined her preferred learning style, I try to tailor my presentation to her preference. I have one friend who is highly literate. We read the Bible together chronologically starting with the story of the creation. She already knew about Jesus but had no foundation to understand why the work of Jesus was necessary. She actually made a profession of faith during the stories of King Saul. I have another friend who fits between the second and third levels. She wants to improve her reading ability. When we study together, she wants to read the Scripture, but then she asks what it means. She still gets her information orally even though she has read the passage. She does not like to attend Bible studies where people read passages and then discuss. She prefers to hear a story.

I have other friends who have never been to school. When I am with them, I tell stories. I don't even try to bring out a book to share with them.

Through the years, as I have worked with Muslim women, I have learned that they don't have a concept of who God is as he has revealed himself through Scriptures. When I talk about Jesus, they automatically reject Jesus, because they have been taught that Christians believe a false doctrine. However, when I start with the beginning of the story—the creation—and let God reveal his character through the stories, I see the women falling in love with God. They are hungry to hear more. They begin to recognize that their relationship is severed and that it is their fault. The Old Testament provides the foundation for understanding why God sent Jesus and for understanding why accepting Jesus is the only way to restore their relationship with God. The Old Testament stories clear the confusion and divide error from truth.

One of my friends had met another missionary and studied the life of Christ with her. After that missionary left, I tried to pick up where she had left off. While my friend liked the stories, she refused to accept Christ. I attended a workshop on CBS and returned determined to try this method, so I started in the Book of Genesis with my friend. We had only reached the stories of Abraham when she made a profession of faith. She needed to have the foundational stories to understand that she was a sinner and that God determined the route to forgiveness.

CBS has several distinguishing characteristics. One major point is that it is a win-win method for evangelizing Muslims. There is no need to enter into arguments. Recently, when I was telling a story of Jesus to a group of women, a visitor—a woman who attends when she is visiting in my area—asked why I was telling stories of Jesus to the group that was all Muslim. She said, "You should be telling them stories about their prophet, Mohammad." I replied by reminding her that we were following the chronology, that we had started with the creation story and that we had arrived at the time of Jesus in the chronological process. This satisfied her. We continued with the story without any argument.

On another occasion, when we were studying the story of Noah, one woman interrupted the story to ask if I believed that Jesus was the Son of God. I stopped, looked at her and said, "You are a Muslim and you have your beliefs; I am a Christian and I have my beliefs, but here we are studying a story that is found in a book that is holy for both of us. That way we can learn more about God without arguing." She said, "Oh." I finished the story of Noah and we discussed what we had learned about God in the story. The women continued to come to the class. I believe that if I had tried to answer this woman with my specific beliefs about Jesus, I would have lost the entire group. They continued to come, and we eventually reached the stories of Jesus. The women continued until they had learned the whole story.

Another important concept is that the chronological process is followed. Future events aren't mentioned. Once an event has happened, it can be referred to again. An example is the sacrifice system. When dealing with the Passover lamb sacrifice, we ask for other examples where God has provided a sacrifice that is a substitute for a human being. The women and girls that I have taught can usually recall these stories correctly and can tell them again. Occasionally when there is a break in the meeting times, I'll give them a teaser to keep their interest, as is done in soap operas that they watch. For example with Joseph's story, we left Joseph in prison just as a school vacation break started. I asked the women to think about what might happen next. Would

Joseph die in prison? Would God save Joseph? What would happen to Joseph's
brothers? Would they ever see each other again? The women laughed at the
questions, but all were in attendance to see what would happen to Joseph
when we restarted the group after the vacation.

The process must be chronological and sequential. Some stories aren't
essential for salvation but need to be told to keep the sequence going and to
help the women keep them in order. One such event is the story of Jacob's family. Enough needs to be told to help the women get from Abraham and Isaac
to Joseph. They need to know who Joseph is and how he is related to Abraham.
The rest of that story would probably be used in discipleship or in dealing with
family issues in the church-planting phase. It is possible to insert stories into the
time line by giving the before and after events which have already been told.
For oral communicators this serves the same function as giving literate communicators a Scripture reference to look up. Occasionally, you will need to
include a story that will be necessary for a later spiritual truth. One example is
the story of the Tabernacle and the curtain that divided the Holy of Holies from
the rest of the building. They need this story to understand the significance of
the tearing of the curtain in the temple when Jesus died on the cross.

Stories are chosen with a purpose. Barriers found in the religion and culture
that keep the individual from accepting Christ must be dealt with. We'll discuss
later how to identify these barriers. In addition, we need to make sure that the
women hear the essential biblical truths necessary for salvation.

The storyteller also chooses the details that are necessary for the person
hearing the story. Then the storyteller writes out the story to make sure that all
details are correct. We can't change the content of the story. What is told
becomes an oral Bible for the person hearing the story. It is possible to short-
en sentences, to use active verbs, to use proper names rather than repeat pro-
nouns and to leave out some details. An example would be, "God told Noah
how high, how wide and how long to build the boat. God told Noah where to
put the window and the door. God told Noah how many levels to make in the
boat. God told Noah how many animals to put in the boat."

Look at the diagram of the Lomé Y on the next page. This is a diagram that
helps you work through the steps in sequence for choosing a story set as well
as the themes that you will want to cover with the story set. There are two sec-
tions of important homework that need to be done before beginning to tell
Bible stories. Once the decision is reached to use CBS, the worker has to
decide which stories to tell. There is a method or a way to determine these. The

Chronological Bible Story Selection
"Lomé Y"

Language et Culture		
Worldview Realities Spiritual Barriers Points of Agreement Perceived needs		

Lostness of Man		
Foundational & Essential Truths for Salvation		

Compiled Track Objectives

1.
2.
3.
(10-15 max.)

Model Bible Story List & Themes	→	**EXAMINE BIBLE STORY LIST**	←	Exhaustive Bible Story List
Time Limitations or Contact Window	→	**Select Trial Story Set**	←	Other Factors: Attention Span Interruptions
Helps Stories	→	**Prepare Story Lessons**	←	Review Dialogue
Teach to Your Coworker	← →	**Test Story Set & Lessons**	← →	Teach to a Small Test Group
Newly Discovered Barriers ----------------- New Objectives	→	**ADJUST LIST** **ADD NEW STORIES** **DELETE UNEEDED STORIES**	←	Objectives Not Completely Covered ----------------- More Than Adequately Covered
SHELL MODEL	→	**MODEL STORY & LESSON SET**	←	ORAL MODEL

Used by permission of Jim Slack

Lomé Y is a schema that describes the entire process. It is something that I have memorized and use as I meet people and decide what stories to use and how.

Before choosing the Bible stories, a thorough world view study needs to be done. The International Mission Board, SBC, has a document that gives a list of suggested questions which will help in determining the worldview. These questions deal with family structure, religion, social structure, politics and financial concerns. In addition, there is a set of questions to help determine the preferred learning style of the target population.

Here are some sample barriers to the gospel that have been found in Paris:

- A woman can't change her religion. She is born a Muslim and will always remain one. (Ruth came from a family that followed the terrible Moabite religion and she changed her religion. Rahab and her family followed the Canaanite religion; the implication is that she changed her religion in marrying one of the Israelites, Salmon.)
- It is possible to hide sins from God.
- Nationality and religion are the same.
- Jesus is a prophet.
- The Bible has been changed.
- Salvation is earned by keeping the basics of the religion and by living a moral life.
- God isn't interested in the individual.
- Folk Islam is widely practiced.
- Husbands and fathers make important decisions for women.
- Women aren't important in the sight of God.
- Religion is external practices rather than a condition of the heart.
- Mohammad is God's prophet and the Koran is God's word.
- Fasting cleanses one from sin.

Knowing these barriers to the gospel and others helps with the story selection. The worldview will also find some bridges in the culture. Some bridges found in Islam include:

- The Torah, the Psalms and the Gospel are the Word of God.
- God is one God.
- The prophets gave us messages from God.
- God expects obedience to His word.

- God speaks through dreams and visions.
- Jesus was born of a virgin.
- God will judge the sins of each person.
- There will be a final judgment.

Another factor that goes into story selection is the essential biblical truths that need to be learned in order to accept Christ as Savior. It is these biblical truths which drive the storying process rather than simply responding to the world-view issues. Some essential truths include:

- God sees and knows everything.
- Nothing is impossible with God. God can change lives.
- God punishes sin.
- God determines the way for salvation.
- Salvation comes through Jesus as the only way.

Neither list is exhaustive, but is only an example of what you need to work with as you pick your stories. After studying the worldview and looking at the essential biblical truths, you are ready to begin picking the barriers and bridges that deal with salvation issues. Some of what you find in a world view needs to be treated in a discipleship track. For example, some issues dealing with folk Islam would be barriers to accepting the gospel and other issues would be discipleship issues. For evangelistic stories, pick the barriers and truths that deal with salvation. Determine the exact points that need to be learned in order for an individual to accept Christ. These points become your objectives.

In addition to the objectives, you need to determine your story themes or the points that you will bring out in many of the stories to reach the objectives. One theme that I have used is the characteristics of God. I have found that the women don't know who God really is. Therefore, with each story, I ask them what they have learned about God in that story. Another theme that I try to bring out is that God determines what is acceptable to him. God tells me what is acceptable rather than me offering something to God that I think he will like. Some people like to use the theme of the sacrifice system that God ordained. I also like to focus on God's promises and that he always keeps his promises. I frequently ask the women to listen for a promise during the story. After the story, I ask them to tell me the promise and if God kept the promise. Then I ask them what this teaches them about God.

Now it's time to begin to pick a list of stories. There are some model lists that already exist. One such model is the book, *God and Woman* by J.O. Terry. In this book, Terry provides 90 stories as a sample evangelistic story track for working with Muslim women. There are good lists of all the Bible stories. You need to consider the age and sex of the group you are teaching as well as the literacy level. Since there is no expositional teaching with the first level of oral communication, this group will need many stories to cover the objectives. A highly literate group will need fewer stories because they can enjoy lessons with expositional teaching and follow the points being taught. You might use some stories for a children's group and choose some different ones with a group of teenage girls while changing again for a group of adult women. For example, I would use the story of Rahab with women and the story of Naaman with men to illustrate the truth that salvation comes by following God's commands to the letter or by total obedience. With children, I use the action stories such as David and Goliath and Daniel and the Lion's Den, whereas with women, I use the stories of Hannah, Ruth and the two widows that Elijah and Elisha helped.

Once you have picked your story list, you need to try it out. With a colleague, I picked a story list and began to tell the stories. I learned that I had left out some important points. Also, some that had seemed terribly important when I picked them, really weren't necessary for the evangelism track. As I taught through the story list, I realized that the story of Joseph's forgiveness of his brothers was a very important one for Muslims. I changed the story list to allow more time to focus on this story. Other stories, especially from the life of Jesus, needed to be told but later in the track. For example, the story of Nicodemus and the story of the Samaritan woman need to come later in the life of Jesus rather than right at first.

Other factors to consider in choosing the list include:

· The number of times you can meet with a group.

· Interruptions that might occur such as holidays or school vacations.

· Literacy level of the group, which affects the number of stories needed.

Once you have your suggested story list, you need to find a group or even an individual and begin to teach it. With my team, I have taught children, teenagers and adult women as groups and also worked with individual women who range from totally illiterate to highly literate. As we have worked with the stories, we have modified the list and now have a model story set that we use most of the time. Below is a revised story list which I compiled with colleagues in 2001 for use with Muslim women in Paris. It has been developed from the original through testing and will continue to evolve as we teach the stories to groups and individuals.

Each story teaches something about God. The repeating themes are: the characteristics of God (God keeps His promises, God provides, God is just, God doesn't tolerate sin, God is all-powerful and all-knowing, God seeks a relationship with man/woman), the acceptable sacrifice, the care God provides for women, the sin nature and the promise of a Savior.

1.   Introduction: Talk about the characteristics of God.
2.   The Creation Story: Everything was perfect and good.
3.   Angels and the fall of Satan: (Isaiah 14:12-14, Ezekiel 28:11-19) An explanation for the presence of Satan and evil spirits in the world.
4.   Adam and Eve's sin and the consequences: God knows everything.
5.   Cain and Abel: God knows everything. God warns the individual.
6.   Noah and the Flood: God doesn't tolerate sin. God provides salvation.
7.   The Tower of Babel: Disobedience to God's command has consequences.
8.   Abraham's call, his walk of faith with God: Abraham had faith, but he wasn't sinless.
9.   Ishmael's birth and life, the birth of Isaac: God keeps His promises.
10. Sacrifice of Isaac: God provides the acceptable sacrifice.
11. Summary of the lives of Isaac and Jacob, including the birth of Jacob's children: God keeps His promises. (This is a linking story to identify Joseph and the promise made to Abraham.)
12. Joseph, from birth to his experience with Potiphar's wife: God was with Joseph everywhere. Even though each person has a sin nature, the act of sinning is a choice.
13. Joseph's experiences in prison, his dreams, Joseph's rise to second in command in Egypt: God stayed with Joseph. God keeps His promises.
14. The famine, the reconciliation of Joseph with his brothers: God desires that we forgive each other and have reconciliation.
15. Summary of the 400 years, the life and call of Moses: God doesn't forget His people.
16. God delivers the people from Egypt (include the story of the Passover): God determines the acceptable act for salvation.
17. God directs the people through the desert, the Ten Commandments: God provides. God clearly tells us what he expects.
18. The Law, the rebellion of the people, a summary of the forty years: God saw disobedience and punished it. God keeps His promise.

19. The entry into the Promised Land, Jericho (with an emphasis on the story of Rahab, her faith and her decision to follow God): God expects total obedience. Rahab's choice allowed her to save herself and her family.

20. Ruth (with an emphasis on her decision to follow God): This story—with the story of Rahab—shows that women have the power to make their own choice to follow God.

21. Hannah and the birth of Samuel: Hannah demonstrated her faith in an all-powerful God who doesn't need any help to accomplish His purpose. This story deals with folk Islamic practices.

22. Saul and the witch of Endor: The story teller needs to review why Saul has lost communication with God. This story deals powerfully with folk Islam.

23. David and Bathsheba, enough of David's life to show that he knew the law and chose to disobey: Sin has consequences even when the individual repents.

24. Elijah, Elisha: Each prophet worked with a widow who needed to obey a strange command in faith. Her obedience saved herself and her family. The obedience was her choice.

25. The birth of Jesus, some of the prophecies regarding his birth: God keeps his promises.

26. Baptism of Jesus, temptation of Jesus: This begins a series of stories that teach who Jesus is.

27. Jesus calms the storm, Jesus feeds the 5000: He is more powerful than nature.

28. Jesus helps the Gaderene demoniac: He is more powerful than evil spirits.

29. Jesus heals the woman sick for twelve years, Jesus raises of the daughter of Jairus: He is more powerful than sickness and death.

30. Jesus interacts with the adulterous woman at the house of Simon, Jesus heals the man with the four friends: He has the power to forgive sins.

31. Jesus and the Samaritan woman.

32. From Palm Sunday to the Last Supper.

33. Arrest, crucifixion and resurrection of Jesus.

34. The ascension, a review of the meaning of the stories told.

35. The story of Lazarus and the rich man, the Judgment Day.

36. Meet with each person individually and ask for a decision.

One group of primary oral communicators is meeting twice a week. This allows for more stories with a better grounding of the essential truths. The teacher uses the stories to teach the women French as well as how to read and write. The women initially come for the literacy class, but many return for the stories. Even when events cause them to miss the literacy portion of the class, they choose to come for the story if possible. One woman from this class has memorized each story. She goes around the neighborhood telling the stories to the women who can't come to the class. We believe that she will tell the stories when she goes back to her home country for her vacation.

CBS is the first evangelistic method that I have used that has allowed me to work with women in groups. The approach is non-aggressive. My prayer is that the whole group will accept Christ and be discipled into a church. One of the advantages of using CBS is that each woman has a good foundation of biblical truth. Once she has completed the evangelism track, taking her from creation through the ascension of Jesus, we start a discipleship track. In the discipleship story track, because she now knows the whole story, we can refer to Jesus in the Old Testament. We can talk about the prophecies as they occur. We can also deal with world view issues that hinder the Christian life. The story track will include some of the original stories but with new themes and some new stories. For example, we will want to talk about family issues and husband/wife relationships. The stories of Isaac and Jacob and their families will be good stories to add. We can also include stories of the different women of the Bible.

As this group forms into a church, we can train the leaders through the stories. We can deal with specific community needs through the telling of these Bible stories. The form of the service will be different. Rather than reading a Scripture passage, the church leader will select a Bible story, tell the group where it is located in relation to the other stories and then tell it. The leader will then lead the group into a discussion of the story and its application to their lives today. All through the use of CBS, a group can be evangelized, discipled, formed into a church with training for the leaders and can begin to plant new church groups.

The storyteller must decide whether or not to use pictures or other aids to help with the story telling. With children, we have used flannel graph. We've used a combination of teaching aids with teenage girls. I have used pictures with women, but the major concern is that they be able to reproduce what they have heard. I don't want them to believe that they must have a picture to tell a story. One colleague in West Africa uses something from the house or village as a story focus or aid in recall. For example, she might use a bowl of fruit with the story of Adam and Eve. With the story of Saul and the witch of Endor, she uses a piece of cloth to disguise herself. For Abraham and Isaac, she uses a butcher knife. With the Samaritan woman's story, she uses a bucket. She believes that the object helps anchor the story, and the use of a common object that is around daily, helps with story recall during the week.

This brief introduction to the basics of CBS does not replace a workshop. There are many possibilities for training in this valuable evangelistic tool. Let me encourage you to consider finding a training session and joining it. It will change your ministry.

Chronological Bible Storying resources are provided by the International Mission Board, SBC, and Southwestern Baptist Theological Seminary. For online resources and information about courses and workshops go to <www.chronologicalbiblestudying.com>.

Annette Hall has worked for twenty-eight years in the Middle East and Western Europe. She uses chronological Bible storying with all her contacts. She is employed by the International Mission Board, Southern Baptist Convention.

Praying for Muslim Women
by Kim Greig

The first step in praying effectively for Muslim women is to see them the way God sees. Every Muslim woman, like you and me, is someone whom God loves. This may seem an obvious statement, but too many of us have held back from praying for and reaching out to Muslims with the love of Jesus because of fear and ignorance. Every Muslim woman is unique and wonderful in God's eyes. We should never presume that they are all the same. There are some important spiritual issues to consider which will help us pray more effectively for them.

The God who sees

The story of Hagar gives us some understanding of how God sees Muslim women. In Genesis 16, we read that Hagar fled into the wilderness after Abram's son Ishmael was conceived. There in the wilderness, after an angel of the Lord told Hagar to return to her mistress, Sarai, Hagar named the place "Beer Lahai Roi," meaning "the God who sees me." Today, Muslim women know God as distant and impersonal—Allah does not see them. But the true character of God is that of one who not only sees them, but also loves them, hears them and weeps over them, not wanting any to perish.

We may also have to be honest and admit that we have not always demonstrated God's heart toward them. We have not heard them or seen them as God does. We may need to repent of our attitudes toward Muslims before we can begin to pray. We need to pray in faith, with a heart of compassion.

Identity and value

A Muslim woman attains her identity solely through her father or her husband. Her entire world is dominated by men. Their authority covers her in every

aspect of life. The veil is an outward representation of that covering and submission. She dresses modestly to guard the honor of her family—the male
members in particular. A Muslim woman has no identity of her own. Her value
is half that of a man: countless rules and regulations keep her in an inferior
position. In praying for the Muslim woman, however, it is important to realize
that men are not the enemy. The true enemy is Satan who comes to rob women
of their identity and value in Christ (John 10:10).

The stronghold of fear

Fear is one of the greatest strongholds for a Muslim woman. She fears being
mistreated, beaten or divorced from her husband. She fears infertility, her mother-in-law, gossip, religious leaders and religious police. Her world beset with the
utter vulnerability of being a woman under Islam, she may seek refuge in folk
Islamic practices which include invoking blessings from dead Muslim saints
and appeasing evil spirits which control many aspects of daily life.

From slaves

Galatians 4:22 tells us that Ishmael was born as a result of works resulting in
slavery. Islam means submission. A Muslim woman understands that she is a
servant of Allah, a servant of her husband and a servant to her brothers and
sons. A Muslim can only relate to God from the position of a servant or slave. A
Muslim must earn salvation through good works. As Christians, through Jesus,
we move from being slaves to sons and daughters (Galatians 4:7). Muslims
need an understanding of repentance and forgiveness through the work of
grace done on the Cross of Calvary.

. . .To daughters

It is very difficult for a Muslim woman to think of God as Father. The very idea
of Jesus being the Son of God is offensive to them and can only be fully
grasped through a revelation by the Holy Spirit. Islam has 99 names for Allah;
"Father" is not one of them. We must pray that Muslim women will know God
as Father.

*Kim Greig has ministered among Muslims throughout South Asia and the Middle East
since 1979. Kim and her husband, Keith, are the International Coordinators of an
international prayer ministry known as '30 Days Muslim Prayer Focus.' This ministry
is now one of the largest focused prayer events in the history of the church, with more
than thirty million Christians participating each year around the world. The Greigs
are currently based in Australia.*

Developing a Ministry to Refugees

by Chérie Rempel

When we envision cross-cultural ministry, we often think it takes place in far away countries. Yet God has brought the mission field to our doorstep in the form of refugee communities in Western nations. Why should we minister to these refugees? Throughout the Old Testament, God commanded his people to treat foreigners fairly, with love, care and charity. He even instructed that they be included in religious festivals. In both the Old and New Testament, God commands us to share with those who do not know Jesus as Lord and clearly states that there will be representatives from all peoples in heaven.

So how do we reach out to these whom God has brought to live in countries not their own? We have many opportunities to meet the needs of foreigners. My suggestions specifically address the needs of refugee women and children.

Crossing cultural barriers with friendship

Invite foreign friends to your home, serving them generously with food and appropriate beverages. Visit them in their homes—your visit to them is considered an honor and is valued even more than an invitation to your home. Remember these guests are like any other women. Learn to appreciate them as friends and seek to earn their love and trust.

Observe carefully how they offer hospitality when you are a guest in their homes so that you can understand cultural differences. To avoid offense, be sure to eat and drink some of every food you are given (unless you have a doctor's orders to avoid it). Learn to cook and enjoy the same foods your refugee friends enjoy, and if you are having a friend for dinner, don't feel compelled to prepare it all yourself. Ask a neighbor to come over and help you.

Special circumstances are special opportunities to visit and thus show support to your friends. Visit them when they are in the hospital, and give them your condolences when a family member dies. Attend their weddings and picnics. To learn more about the culture of your refugee friends, observe carefully how they dress—both the style and modesty of their clothing. Note also how they act, especially in relation to men, and follow their example. For instance, you may take your shoes off in their homes, cross your legs differently, and avoid talking at length with men. When you don't know how to do something, ask! They will be delighted to explain their culture and customs to you.

Helping with physical needs

Most refugees will have food stamps. You can also help them register for Thanksgiving and Christmas food baskets, but be aware that they may not like some American foods. Ideas for food baskets or gifts for Middle Easterners include fresh or dried fruit, vegetables, potatoes, large bags of nuts or seeds in their shells, dried chick peas, yellow lentils, frozen chicken or turkey (no pork products), white flour, white sugar, white rice, salt, vegetable oil, gelatin, pudding and cake mixes.

Introduce your friends to your favorite places to shop, like department stores, warehouse stores, or ethnic stores. They may not be familiar with how to use coupons or understand sale advertising, so this is another area in which you can offer practical assistance. Many refugees are glad to have used furniture and some are glad to have used clothing. Possible sources include attics, basements, church "stores," garage sales, thrift stores and even roadside "cast-offs" in wealthier neighborhoods.

As a general rule, it is better not to loan money. If you do loan it, consider it a gift. If you give to one needy person, others will expect a similar gift. Instead, help your friends open a checking or savings account, and teach them to write checks, balance their checkbook and use ATM or debit cards. Discourage them from getting or using a credit card.

Navigating bureaucracy

There are many benefits available to refugees, but they may not have the skills needed to take advantage of them. You may want to talk to their social workers to learn more about what your friends are required to do: they may need to take ESL classes, do volunteer work or hunt for a job and work for pay. Your friends may need assistance filling out paperwork for food stamps, Medicaid, green cards, work authorization, work applications, driving permits and other documents. Discourage any dishonesty in filling out these forms, as that will only cause problems for them later.

Initially many refugees have Medallion health. Help them take advantage of it. Encourage them to get check-ups and immunizations for their children. Persuade pregnant women and new mothers to go for exams and advise them to go to the dentist. Some children and mothers qualify for WIC supplements of cereal, milk, peanut butter, cheese, eggs and other food items.

You can also offer assistance in applying for Section 8 and public housing. It will usually be less expensive than conventional housing at thirty percent of their adjusted income. This will enable them to rent a larger apartment, instead of one that barely meets their needs.

Education for children and adults

To extend your friendship to refugees, consider organizing a class to teach a hobby, such as sewing, cooking or cake decorating. You can offer the class to refugee women, or make it into a summer club for their children. Allow time for refreshments and socializing.

Encourage your friends to attend county or church classes teaching English as a second language, especially if it's required by the welfare or social services office or if the government will pay for them to attend. As an alternative, you could teach refugees in small classes in their own apartment complex or as individuals in their homes. Some women may know how to speak but are not literate. Also, you could organize an English club for children or teenagers and help them with their homework.

You may be able to find appropriate day care for children of working parents or your refugee friends may need your aid in getting their children registered for school. This will involve paperwork, shots at the doctor's office, and possibly providing transportation to accomplish these things. Instruct the children regarding where to meet the bus. Preschool children should be registered for Head Start; children with learning disabilities may need you to facilitate their entry into special education classes by communicating with the teacher or principal. School nurses may also provide names of doctors who will treat refugees for a reduced fee.

Classes in English as a Second Language(ESL)

If you choose to teach an ESL or conversation class, use English as the language of instruction. Be friendly, letting your refugee friends know that you are glad they are in your country. Don't use a lot of lectures and explanations; instead, speak slowly and give examples of what you want the students to do. Challenge your students without discouraging them with material that is too difficult for them. Praise your students when they make progress, and correct them when they make errors. Broken English, unnatural speech and idioms will hinder communication with your students, but feel free to use a lot of objects, illustrations, pantomime and gestures. Continue to review and repeat lessons before moving on to something new.

The Bible may be used in class, but carefully, as words in the Bible can be easily misunderstood. Starting with Old Testament stories, you may explain about sin and the system of sacrifice leading to Christ's substitutionary atonement for our sin. Avoid difficult theological issues until you've established a deep relationship of trust with your refugee friends. If asked a difficult question, instead of answering the question directly, counter with a question such as, "What do you think?"

Maintain a balance between active teaching and active learning, allowing the students themselves to speak and write. Your students can work together in pairs or small groups before you ask them to perform before the whole class. Make the lessons interesting by teaching things they need or want to know.

Work and transportation

Refugees naturally arrive with the expectation of doing the same kind of work they did in their former home country; however that may not be possible until they get the appropriate schooling and licensing in their new countries. You can help them adjust their expectations for work. Potential places of employment may be hotels, hospitals, airports, rental car agencies, car factories, ethnic restaurants, clothing stores, delivery agencies or schools.

Many of your friends will be able to get around with the bus system after you teach them how to buy tokens. If a refugee friend asks you to teach her how to drive, do so in her car. (If she doesn't have access to a car, learning to drive will not be a very useful skill!) Be a patient teacher. The Department of Motor Vehicles will provide information about traffic laws. Be sure to acquaint your friends with seat-belt and car-seat laws.

Addressing spiritual needs

Through your friendship and the assistance you offer your refugee friends, the Lord will give you opportunities to witness to them. As the Lord gives you spiritual fruit, Bible story telling and Bible studies are means of discipling women and children. If you have parental consent, another way to disciple children is to host a five-day club, sponsored by Child Evangelism Fellowship, in your home.

Prayer is another avenue for addressing your friends' spiritual needs. Pray with your friends in the name of Jesus when they are sick or have problems. Pray aloud and praise the Lord with them when God answers!

You may want to share with your friends that you have befriended them and helped them as an act of obedience to the Bible. If it seems appropriate, and if you've established a relationship of trust and acceptance with them, give them a Scripture portion, tract, Christian biography or testimony in their language. Be prepared to answer their questions in a way that they can understand.

Where does ministry to refugees lead? By reaching out to Muslim refugees, you are obeying God's commands, establishing friendships with people who may not know any other Westerners and helping them with physical needs. This in turn opens their hearts for you to address the needs of which they are not aware—their spiritual needs. By being a friend you are opening up doors for communicating the gospel in an environment of trust.

Suggested Resources for Teaching ESL to Refugees

Azar, Betty S. *Basic English Grammar. Fundamentals of English Grammar. Understanding and Using English.* Englewood Cliffs, N.J.: Prentice Hall Regents, 1984.
Grammar exercises, low, low intermediate and intermediate, respectively.

Brown, H. Douglas. *New vistas.* Upper Saddle River, N.J.: Prentice Hall Regents, 1999.
Five levels of student conversation textbooks and three levels of listening tapes, especially for the student with some academic interest.

Carver, Tina K., and others. *A Writing Book: English in Everyday Life.* 2nd ed. Upper Saddle River, N.J.: Prentice Hall Regents, 1998.
A teachers resource book of writing activities.

Foley, Barbara, and Howard Pomann. *Lifelines: Coping Skills in English.* Upper Saddle River, N.J.: Prentice Hall Regents, 1993.
Four levels of student conversation books, especially for refugees in the USA.

Nishio, Yvonne, *Longman ESL literacy.* Longman, 1991.
A student book good for teaching literacy to students who have some knowledge of writing.

The Oxford Picture Dictionary (1998), Oxford University Press.
A good resource for teaching vocabulary.

Rempel, Chérie. Contextualized/simplified Bible stories and other reading activities.

Reading activities available at 8079 Barcarole Ct., Springfield, VA 22153-2945 or at cjrempel@cs.com.

Especially for literacy:

Molinsky, Steven J., and Bill Bliss. Access: *Fundamentals of Literacy and Communication*. Englewood Cliffs, N.J.: Prentice Hall Regents, 1990.
A good resource for teaching literacy to students who have little or no knowledge of writing.

Molinsky, Steven J., and Bill Bliss. *Word by Word Basic Literacy Workbook*, White Plains, N.Y.: Prentice Hall Regents, 1999.
Use in conjunction with the dictionary; for students who already have some knowledge of writing.

Molinsky, Steven J., and Bill Bliss. *Word by Word Basic Picture Dictionary*. White Plains, N.Y.: Prentice Hall Regents, 1997.
A dictionary to be used in conjunction with the *Word by Word Basic Literacy Workbook*.

Chérie Rempel has worked among the same Middle Eastern people group since 1992 in their homeland and in two Western countries. She has a master of arts in Teaching English as a Foreign Language from Columbia International University and has used ESL throughout her ministry.

Church planting in the Muslim World: A Personal Account

by Meg Ritchie

The role of a church-planter is not a static one, but one that changes as the church itself is formed and matures. This paper will recount my personal experiences which demonstrate the evolving role of the church-planter. Illustrations span a period of sixteen years from 1966, when we arrived in our area of ministry, to 1982, when we were forced to leave the country.

The growth of the church in this country has been phenomenal since 1982. Two and a half years ago, after a separation of seventeen years, we had the opportunity to see some of our national brothers again. They recounted that in their area alone, thirty-five churches had been planted. "But then we've been away for two weeks, so that may have changed!" they said.

According to their estimate there were 12 thousand Christians country-wide in January 1999. One government official has stated that the populace is converting to Christianity at the rate of six a day and has asked the national assembly to take action.

It wasn't always like that. When my husband and I first arrived in the capital city, Christian workers had maintained a steady witness for over eighty years. We were untrained compared to those going overseas today. Because we weren't sure of our goals, we joined a team of four other more experienced workers.

Group formation

Several other groups were working in the city, so we decided to join forces and bring our contacts to one meeting place. As a result, we soon had a large group of mostly unbelievers with varying motives for being together. When the police got curious and began to investigate, the group dwindled to a core of young people who were either believers or serious seekers. The smaller meeting began to take on a different flavor. When we contacted correspondence course students, we found that some had already trusted in Christ. They joined the group, forming a nucleus of serious, relatively unafraid believers.

The church was diverse in terms of both theology and ethnicity. The majority of those who attended were single men and women, an older man, a mother of five children, and other adults. There was both a spirit of unity and a joy in being together as the Holy Spirit helped us overcome our differences.

Training of believers

After some years, the group numbered about fifty, including several Westerners. Services were in French and Arabic. In addition to discipleship and teaching, activities included social gatherings, Sunday school, monthly outings, fellowship meals, prayer meetings planned by the church, spontaneous prayer groups, summer camps and weekend conferences. Training was provided on how to teach children's classes, as well as teaching on Christian marriage, the occult, meat sacrificed to idols, baptism, the church and the role of suffering in the life of a believer. Theological education by extension classes were another way believers were equipped. Courses included introduction to the Old Testament, introduction to the New Testament, basic doctrine, Acts, Romans, and church history.

Subsequent to the study "What is the Church?," elders were elected. Three foreigners served with four national deacons. This leadership functioned for two years; later the number of foreigners was reduced to one. At the end of two years, the last foreigner resigned, only preaching or teaching at the request of the national leadership. The group met in a store-front downtown, handling its own affairs including its own finances. A few months after church leadership became entirely indigenous, foreigners were asked to leave the country; God's timing was perfect.

Planning for the process

In midst of the formation of this church, our team and mission began examining our gifts and defining our goals for believers and churches. Our profile of an ideal national believer was, as follows:

· He realizes that God has a plan for his life. He puts Christ first and takes steps to separate himself from sin.

- He has a consistent daily devotional time and is developing his prayer life.
- He demonstrates faithfulness and a desire to learn and apply the Word of God through regular Bible study and scripture memory. He has completed one TEE course, where feasible, and has memorized 60 verses.
- He understands the biblical teaching of the ministry of the Holy Spirit in his life.
- He manifests a heart for witnessing, feeling a special responsibility to witness within the family circle, and is able to give his testimony and present the gospel clearly.
- He attends church and maintains close ties with the local fellowship, displaying love, unity, responsibility and loyalty to the local fellowship.
- He demonstrates a servant heart in his sincere interest in helping others.
- He distinguishes the elements of Islamic teaching which are contrary to biblical revelation and abstains from participation in aspects of his culture which are anti-Christian.
- He understands the importance of baptism.
- He has stood the test of persecution for the name of Christ.
- He is a learner, open and teachable.

Who of us could fit this description?

We then had to identify what we were looking for in a national church and define our role in the process. Does a group of ladies being taught by a foreigner constitute a church? Is a group of teenagers meeting and growing together in a foreigner's home a church? There was never any doubt that we were trying to work ourselves out of a job, but at what point? We wrote a document describing the goal toward which we were working and praying. The main elements were as follows:

- At least ten baptized believers
- Families
- Locally recognized leaders
- Meeting place
- Able to care for its own finances

Often groups start in foreign workers' homes. We had large groups meeting in several foreigners homes for years, especially during the week. This gave us the opportunity to be hospitable until there were other possibilities. Security issues needed to be considered in choosing the place of meeting.

Modeling

When we were in candidate school back in 1960, an elderly gentleman challenged us, declaring, "Each of us should be able to say, 'If you want to know what Jesus is like, come to my house!'"

Because the main role of the church planter is modeling, the worker must be sure he is a good model to follow. A significant number of foreigners usually are involved in this formation stage of a church.

Without exception, the workers on the church-planting team had open homes. Their homes held church activities and served as places to eat, sleep, cry or seek counsel. I recently asked our forty-one-year-old son if he had ever minded the number of people we had in the house. His reply: "Never. That was the fun of it all."

At one point we wanted to discern the feelings of the group about the presence of foreigners and suggested that it might be a good idea if we pulled out. The response was immediate and helpful to us: "Yes, [you may pull out] if you can show us where in the Scriptures it says that a church should be made up of one nationality." We ourselves felt that the presence of such a variety of foreigners helped us model what a church is rather than just teaching about it.

It is obvious that the role of church-planter evolves. First the worker is an evangelist, then trainer and discipler. Gradually he becomes a partner and then an observer. Finally he exits the scene. In each stage he is a model to be imitated.

Baptism and the Lord's Supper

Teaching on these should come soon after conversion. Our policy, however, was to teach and wait until the individual believers asked for baptism. Baptism confirms to the family and often to the police that this person is really serious and has become a traitor to his community and country. We did not want to pressure anyone to take this step until he was able to face the consequences.

We learned that preparation classes were necessary for believers to understand the biblical meaning of baptism. In the early stages foreigners did the baptizing, but that soon changed. In one country parents baptized their own children. We baptized in the sea, in a lake, in a desert stream, in bathtubs and once in a leaking baptistry!

While the church was very young, we reserved the Lord's Table for private meetings of the baptized; non-believers who attended the worship meetings sometimes mocked and giggled in disrespect. Our policy varied to fit the circumstances and exceptions were made.

Money

Tithing and stewardship must be taught at the appropriate moment, but what should be done with the money? Should it be spent on needs within the group? These questions should be decided by the group of baptized believers. They see and understand the consequences of giving in the context of their culture better than we do. One group decided that no money would be spent on members but used for the poor and outside ministries. Another group decided that, because its members were too poor, the funds could be used for medicines as the need arose within the group. Making their own financial decisions confirms to the group that the church belongs to them.

Funds coming from outside the country, even though they were donated to help the church by well-intentioned people, often caused jealousy and division. Who should receive scholarships or funds to attend conferences or to study abroad is also a sticky question. If possible, it is advantageous to set up comparable study programs within the country. Many more people can benefit from the courses and the lessons can be adapted to the needs at hand.

Preparing believers for persecution

The new believer may experience isolation from his family and friends. The church needs to replace that family in any way it can, at least until the initial violent reactions subside. Foreigners were able to model a biblical response to persecution as many were summoned to the police on numerous occasions. However, foreigners only faced the possibility of expulsion. National believers were never sure what would transpire during their interrogations. Some of them gave tremendous testimony to the Lord's faithfulness while they faced police or other authorities. Often the police were invited to come to the meetings to see for themselves what was going on.

The Scriptures guide our behavior with many verses on this topic: "If the world hates you, keep in mind that it hated me first" (John 15:18). "When you are brought before ... authorities, do not worry about how you will defend yourelves, ... for the Holy Spirit will teach you at that time what you should say" (Luke 12:11-12). "If you suffer as a Christian, do not be ashamed, but praise God that you bear that name (1 Peter 4:16). "For our struggle is not against flesh and blood, but against ... the powers of this dark world ..." (Eph 6:12). "But I tell you: Love you enemies and pray for those who persecute you ..." (Matt. 5:44).

Discipleship

We sometimes discipled one-on-one, but felt that discipling in groups was more effective. The convert often learns from others in his group as much as he learns from the teacher; and he sees that he is not alone. However, group discipleship may not always be possible, especially where an underlying cultural distrust of others is present. My husband worked alone with the son of an imam for five years before he was willing to meet another believer. Even after he had a clear conversion experience, he still shied away from meeting others. But the very first time he met other young men, he led the lesson time.

Church activities themselves were training experiences. The foreign elders worked closely with the Muslim-background believers who were deacons as well as other national believers, involving them in leading worship services, running the church library, performing special music, teaching children, leading Bible studies and prayer meetings, and eventually preaching.

Marriage and family

Our constant prayer was not so much that God would convert whole families, but that he would form Christian families from the young people who were already active in the church. God answered those prayers abundantly. Two members of a soccer team who converted in 1981 recently told us, "When we came to Christ . . . there were no Christian women—not even the shadow of one. Now look and see how faithful the Lord is. We all have Christian wives and we each have two children."

Conclusion

If I were to identify the elements which are absolutely necessary for the success of a church-plant, I would say faith, love and prayer. We should ask ourselves, "Do I really believe God will bring people to himself and mold them together into a strong, united body? Do I love the people I work with and the people I work among?" Neither fluency in the language, nor possessing numerous gifts are worth much without love. And finally, "Are we people of prayer?"

Meg Ritchie and her husband have been involved in church planting in several countries in the Muslim world. They have now retired.

Muslim Women and the Media

by Ana

In many Muslim societies, women are confined to the home and live separate lives from their male relatives. Within those walls they live in hopelessness and fear with few liberties. For some, their only contact with the outside world is radio, books, and perhaps television—all potential tools to reach their hearts and minds with the life-changing message of Father God. In fact, modern media can provide immediate access to new audiences around the world and is one method God has given his church to communicate with the remaining unreached 50 percent of the world's population. I am convinced that radio, and media in general, are God's mighty tools for world evangelization today, particularly among Muslim women.

Communication is crucial in God's design for human history

"In the beginning was the Word, and the Word was with God, and the Word was God" (John 1:1). Every time the Word was spoken, the miracle of creation happened. The writer of Hebrews adds to the picture by revealing to us the greater scope of God's infinite power as God the Father speaks through God the Son "who being the brightness of His glory and the express image of His person, and upholding all things by the word of his power … sat down at the right hand of the Majesty on high" (Hebrews 1:3, KJV).

There are three principles to consider as we talk about communicating the Word of God:

- God not only created all things through the power of his word, but also has been upholding the universe with his word ever since.
- While the Genesis account tells us that everything was made by the word, man and woman were created for the word. Adam's first job was to name all living creatures. Every baby is born into the world with this God-given abili-

ty to communicate with others. Communication is the main skill humans
have to pass on their history, knowledge, science, culture, art, information, and
technology.

· Man was given not only the ability to communicate with other humans, but
also to communicate with God and to live in communion with him. The Fall
of Adam and Eve caused sin to enter the human heart and severed this relationship. Through the ages, God has sought man by different means, especially through his revealed Word. Romans 10:17 states: "Consequently, faith
comes from hearing the message, and the message is heard through the
Word of Christ." Paul makes this powerful statement after having raised a key
question: "And how can they believe in the one of whom they have not
heard?" (Romans 10:14b).

New paradigms in world missions

When the Great Commission was given, there were 200 million people living
on Planet Earth. Today we have passed the six billion mark. Fifty percent are still
out of the reach of the conventional missionary enterprise. For decades missionaries, many of whom were women, have gone to Africa, Asia and the
Middle East taking the life-changing message of Jesus to the Muslim world.
Many have lost their lives on the mission field. We honor them, as well as those
who are still taking the message wherever the Lord leads them.

With the increasing population growth in the Islamic world, it is obvious that
there is a need to act strategically and to be willing to change and adapt our
missionary paradigms; otherwise, the question will remain unanswered:"…how
can they believe in the one of whom they have not heard?" God never gives us
a command without giving us the means to fulfill it. During the past century,
he has given a new tool to his disciples.

Why radio?

In this presentation I will contain myself to the subject of radio to reach
Muslim women, because radio has been the tool with which I have served my
Lord for over 30 years, first in my native country of Brazil, then in Asia and now
all over the world.

Why is radio an effective medium? First, it is readily available. Even in the
poorest countries of Indochina and beyond, the ratio of available radio
receivers is one for every five people. Though radio is very personal, it reaches
the masses, crossing geographical, cultural, political, social and ideological bar-

riers. If the message is presented by a speaker who has perfect command of the language and an understanding of the target audience, the results are phenomenal!

Homes which would never be open to a missionary are open to radio. Radio is a private companion of those who are fearful and lonely. Many who would never step into an evangelical church, eagerly turn on their radios day after day to hear Christian broadcasts. I met a young lady in New Jersey who was born and raised in Egypt. In her teen years she listened to programs while hiding a little transistor radio under her pillow.

One superpower radio broadcast can reach more people in fifteen minutes than the Apostle Paul reached in his lifetime! It covers more territory in those fifteen minutes than the average missionary could cover in many months. It can communicate in many languages. One organization's broadcasts, for example, are in more than 160 languages. Radio programming can be tailor-made to suit different audiences—children, youth, women and the general public. I have produced programs for women living in Muslim, Buddhist, and animistic societies, for large groups in Indonesia, Cambodia and other countries. Radio is a teacher of congregations without a pastor and a trailblazer that facilitates church growth. I have seen churches formed around the radio in the Amazon jungles as well as in Asia.

Radio and Muslims

Radio is especially effective in Muslim cultures that lean heavily on oral tradition. History, family stories, feasts, reports of war, even prescriptions of herbal medicine continue to be passed on orally from generation to generation, especially among illiterates in rural areas.

The religious life of these Muslims is based on what they hear; therefore, radio is ideal to communicate religious truths. Because the Muslim listener cannot argue with a broadcast, radio provides the unique opportunity to examine beliefs in the privacy and secrecy of home.

Lastly, it is important to remember radio's consistent availability. It is never sick, never tired, never moody nor unwilling to talk! Even if it finds resistence at first, it is a friendly voice already inside the listener's home, willing to minister to the sincere seeker, day after day, rain or shine.

How will Muslim women believe?

It has been said that women in the 10/40 Window could very well be the largest unreached people group on earth today. Of the three billion women in the world, 23 percent are Muslims—that's one out of every four. (If we put them shoulder to shoulder, we could wrap the world four and a half times.) Most of them live segregated in their own homes, unable to come and go as they please, oppressed by a culture which discriminates against them and strips them of their dignity and value as human beings.

Before we discuss the effectiveness of media in reaching out to Muslim women, we need to remember the importance of prayer. Prayer will soften these women's hearts to receive the Word of God. Without the power of the Holy Spirit touching their lives and instilling hope in midst of their hopelessness, convicting them of their sins and their need of eternal salvation through Jesus Christ alone, all that we say or do will be of no eternal value. The most important task we are called to do is to shake the gates of hell by our prayers on behalf of the souls of these dear women. It has been said that "prayer is the work; ministry is reaping the results."

But for whom are we praying? We need to know how ministry to Muslim women is different from ministry to other women. In most Islamic cultures, women are kept away from schools and the workplace. In some Muslim countries, the law gives women the right to work outside their homes. However, since the marketplace is dominated by males, women have few or no opportunities to participate. Women remain subject to their male relatives and, as such, their activities are restricted and their opportunities to be exposed to the gospel, limited. Robbed of their personal freedom, they are kept away from strangers, particularly foreigners, and certainly from any Christian influence.

Women make up half of the world's population. In Indonesia, the largest Muslim country in the world, women make up 56 percent of the population, yet their participation in society, apart from raising their children, is minimal. In some countries, a mother loses control of her sons when they turn seven years of age. Women do not have the right to their own lives and families. Ignored by their fathers, scorned by their brothers, and abused by their husbands, they face a multitude of emotional, physical, intellectual, social, and—most of all—spiritual problems. Most of them live in hell on earth and will live in hell for all eternity if they do not believe in Jesus Christ, the only one who can deliver them from evil. But " . . . how can they believe in the one of whom they have not heard?"

Many Muslim women cannot read or write. Sixty-six percent of the illiterates of the world are women. In societies where boys are celebrated, girls do not have the "luxury" of education, thus illiteracy among them is high. Unable to read even a simple piece of Christian literature, Paul's question still remains, especially for Muslim women, "And how can they believe in the one of whom they have not heard?"

Though isolation, discrimination, and illiteracy restrict these women, they are the gatekeepers of the home. One organization's Arabic Ministry Director said: "All too often we have minimized the role of women in Arab society. They hold the keys to the home, and the home is the core of Arab society. Therefore the key to impacting Arab society with the Christian message is its women. We need to reach out to Arab women, not because they are in a dire situation—though they may be—but because of the unique role and influence they have in their homes."

Women are the key to society. In my travels around the world, researching the plight of women, talking to them in the markets, in their homes, and on the streets, I have come to realize that women are very influential people!

Muslim women, however, face a distinct set of paradigms dictated by their Islamic belief system, independent of their country of origin. As in any other culture, the communication of the message we preach must be contextualized in order to be relevant and easily understood. We must begin with what they understand. Monotheism, for example, could be a stepping-stone. In addition, the person of Isa in the Koran—who is the Jesus of the Bible—can be the starting point for sharing what the Bible has to say about him. Many of the moral laws in the Koran stem from the Torah (Old Testament). Muslims accept the final judgment. They acknowledge sin and God's holiness.

The most important thing to remember is love. The love of God, lavishly poured out in our hearts, should be the very fabric of any ministry to Muslim women. Love must be the essence of our work and the only driving force of our ministry.

Conclusion

"And how can they believe in the one of whom they have not heard?" In his grace and mercy, the sovereign God, creator of the universe, the incarnate Word, has given to our generation not only a command and a message but also the means to proclaim it in unprecedented ways. Now they can hear!

Radio has been called "the quiet revolution." Through its message, lives are changed one by one, and the coming of our King Jesus is hastened. The Great Commission can be accomplished if the Church accepts and integrates the media—especially radio—into its strategic missionary planning and execution. Women in the 10/40 Window, living in difficult-to-access countries, can depend on this powerful "missionary" disguised in the form of a small radio receiver. Yes, they will believe in Jesus Christ, communicate with him, and find strength and hope as daughters of the King, because now they can hear!

Excerpts from Muslim listeners' letters
From a loving mother

Thank you so much for your letter, which came three months ago. I have been trying to follow the guidelines you have given to me. My only connection with Jesus is prayer. I ask him to help me in this difficult life. There are so many difficulties and struggles here. Your messages are very comforting to my soul and spirit. Every time I listen to your program it seems as if my heart is filled with hope and faith, especially when you share the testimony of others. I said yes, it is possible for me as well to give my heart to Jesus, even though I have done so many evil things.

Dear friend, the life here with all the difficulties has become much more joyful because when I hear your program it brings much happiness to me. I am no longer upset about what life will bring for me because I have hope in Jesus.

I have a sick daughter who I have committed to Jesus Christ. I would be grateful if you could pray for my daughter and me. I know Jesus can do miracles and wonders. He has comforted my soul, and I know he is very generous to his children. I have asked him to forgive my sins and help my daughter. We have dedicated our child to Jesus Christ. I am so grateful Jesus was willing to die on the cross for my sin, and we can receive the gift of eternal life. Thank you for sharing the word of God with us.

From a university student

... I have a question I hope you can answer. Does Christ teach that women should wear a chador (covering from head to foot)? Was this something that he felt was important? I am in love with Jesus Christ. I love his teaching and all his words. How could a person, who believes in another religion, convert to Christianity? Do we have to deny the good things from other religions? Finally, please send me a picture of Jesus Christ and his literature, including the gospels. This can be a big help for me.

From an 11-year-old girl

...I have a deep love for your programs and am one of your faithful listeners. Every night I listen to your message of hope. I have encouraged my relatives to listen as well because your programs have a great influence on me.

My religion is complete and worthy to be believed but at the same time I have respect for your religion. I listen to your program because I have a deep desire to know about Christianity. Sometimes I write down the beautiful words of Jesus. I pray that these words would purify me. I sincerely desire to have your holy book and a picture of Jesus Christ ...Could you also tell me why was Jesus crucified? Can you also prove he was actually crucified? ...

From a frightened but brave girl

...I am writing to you with fear because in our culture girls are not permitted to go outside of the home and definitely cannot communicate with strangers. When I have time, I listen to the radio to occupy my mind and my time and forget about my miserable situation. To my surprise I was able to listen to your program. I do not think this was an accident, but that God brought this my way to know about the love of God. Here we do not learn about the love of God. I have come to the conclusion that the God you talk about is very different from the God we are told about in my country. I love your God. I was so excited about your programs that I recorded some of them and shared them with other friends. Now all of my family and others are listening to the cassettes and we have copied them and encouraged others to listen to your programs as well. It is hard for me to believe that God cares about us like you say. I need to experience that. Until now I have only known an unjust lifestyle. Please send me a New Testament.

From a troubled young girl

...Even though I do not like what you are sharing, I continue to listen to your radio programs. You are not sharing anything bad, but when you speak I feel convicted as a sinner before God. I never felt that I was a sinner but rather condemned God for my problems. Now I am learning that it may be my fault. Maybe it is what you call sin that is causing me not to see God's hand in my life. The truth is that I still do not believe I am a sinner ...Even if it is my fault that I do not see God at work, I have not found out what exactly I have done wrong and how I can be rid of it. I would love to know God in the way that you share. Tell me what I should do. How can I grow in my faith in God? Everyone knows that we should believe in God and do good works, but how can we when we do not have the willpower to do this? Even if there is a way to strengthen our faith, society is so evil that it will not allow our faith to grow. In this culture, girls do not have a right to do anything. We feel pressure in every aspect of our life ... (Even in my family there is dictatorship. Every time I ask questions, they merely answer, "Because you are a girl.") Why did God make me a girl? Why did he put a difference between boys and girls? I do not know how to express my feelings, but I do want to thank you for your programs that cause me to think. Please help me to have peace and comfort such as you have....

From a religious lady

I am a very religious person and satisfied with my own religion. I live in the truth that God has given to his prophet. However I have been listening to your program and it has disturbed me. You give a quotation on your programs that you claim is from the gospel. I do not believe this is the word of Jesus when you quote from him, "I am the way the truth and the life, no man comes to the Father except through me." Don't you know that Jesus prophesied that there would be another prophet who would come after him? This is the prophet I am follow-ing. However I respect your teaching and have been listening to learn more about what you believe. As a result I have come to see that there are many things I can agree with you about, but there are other things I cannot agree with you about.

Is the gospel you are sharing the true gospel or has it been changed? ... I would appreciate it if you could send me some of your literature and the gospel you are sharing from, that I may study it myself.

A testimony for the glory of God

By writing down my testimony for you dear people, I want to show you what a great work you have done. When I was about nine years old, my mother began to tell me about Jesus Christ and about the God of love and truth. Every day she would ask me to sit and listen to your radio program. Even when I had homework or did not want to listen, she asked me to listen. She never dreamed she would become a Christian, but she had a deep desire for God.

It was clear to me that the God you talked about was different from the God of Islam. You talked about a God who forgave evil and ugly actions and helped people to live a holy life. This caused me to have a deep desire toward Jesus and his heavenly Father. This situation continued until I was fourteen years old.

Then when I was not able to listen to your program, my mother recorded it for me to listen to it later.

One day, as a friend and I were walking, we stood in front of a church. My friend said, "Let us go into this church." We were both excited to do so, but at the same time we were afraid. At that time I was not interested in becoming a Christian. My friend who was also a Muslim but had been listening to your radio program said, "We should become Christians soon because we could die and we do not want to die in sin." I do not know what came over me at that point, but I began to criticize her and told her that if she became a Christian, God would never forgive her. Because of my persuasion, my friend did not become a Christian.

Ten days later I found myself alone in a church with a deep desire to become a Christian. That same week I received a letter from you dear people with the gospels. You do not know the joy this brought for me. I became willing to go anywhere to come to know Jesus personally. You can not know how much your letter helped me to grow in spiritual faith in Jesus Christ. I decided to pray the prayer that you said on the radio, and I accepted Jesus Christ as my personal Savior. I told my mother that I would follow Jesus Christ.

In just a little while, my entire family, my parents and my sister, became Christians. Then some of our friends became Christians and we became a church in our town. When our relatives found out we had become Christians, they excommunicated us from their circle. Even our friends, who we thought would want to live like Christians and would want to help us and encourage us, left. We Christians united but began to have many difficulties because we believed in Jesus. When you prayed for the listeners on the radio, my family sat together and cried and prayed to God. Our cry was not one of despair but one of hope and joy because we felt that almighty God was with us.

It is simple to accept Jesus as Savior, but it is most important to keep faith in Him. Even though we lost friends and relatives, we were grateful to God for the joy He had given us as a result of salvation. Yes, we know that all our sins have been forgiven and God has given us a new life. When I realized that Christians all over the world are praying for us believers in my country, I was strengthened in my faith.

Now I am twenty-nine years old. Almost fifteen years have passed since I became a Christian. God has given me a husband and a child. We are both active members in a church in another town. We left our hometown because of the pressure and difficulty. God helped us to find a church in another town.

It had always been my dream to meet the radio pastor who helped me to find strength and courage to become a Christian, and then who was always there with his Bible reading and preaching to help my wounded spirit. I wanted to meet him who during this most difficult time in our life always encouraged us and lifted us up with his prayers and helped us keep our faith.

As a result of coming outside of the country for a Christian conference it was a joy to have my dream fulfilled. God heard my prayer so I could meet this dear radio pastor who has helped my family and me greatly. Now dear friends just like you, it is my wish to proclaim the message of Jesus Christ with all my soul and heart and let the people know about the freedom that Jesus can give us from the slavery of Satan. I wish that within the church I could be a good child for Jesus and my heavenly Father who gave me eternal life.

Dear Brethren, please pray for us that we can proclaim the name of Jesus in our country and serve Him. I will kiss the feet of all of you who brought the message of Jesus Christ for my family and me.

Ana works with Project Hannah, a ministry offering compassion and hope to suffering women worldwide, through prayer, awareness and radio programming in their heart language.

Leading Abused and Repressed Muslim Women to Christ

by Hasinoro Raja

South Africa is a multi-cultural country in which male superiority and chauvinism are built into the social structure. Consequently, the incidence of abuse in different forms is high throughout the country. It stretches across ethnic, racial, educational and socio-economic lines. On December 19, 1999, the Sunday Times wrote that "more than forty percent of Cape Town men (of all races) interviewed in a survey by the Medical Research Council admitted they had physically or sexually abused their wives or girlfriends." In 1998, fifty-four thousand rapes were reported. During the first half of 1999, twenty-four thousand rapes were reported. However, the Medical Research Council estimates that only one in every ten rapes is reported. Incredibly, one out of every four baby-girls born throughout this year will eventually be sexually molested. The situation is not helped by the myth that sleeping with young virgins can cure AIDS. As girls today become sexually active at a much younger age, children become victims of sexual abuse.

The Muslims in South Africa come in many varieties. There are those who are disillusioned with Islam, others who are ambivalent about their religion and a large bloc who are content with their beliefs. Each group has gradations. Each group has many victims of abuse. Within that context the Lord led me to put together a series of studies, "Restoring Broken Vessels," to help women reeling from attacks on their bodies and sense of self.

The first time I used those studies at a ladies' conference, I thought only of helping Christian women. But when a Muslim woman who accompanied a Christian friend made a commitment to Christ at the end of that conference, I realized that I had a tool for Muslim outreach. This was confirmed when I was told later that two women used what they had learned at the conference to lead to Christ two of their Muslim friends who had been abused.

This paper contains a synopsis of that series of studies.

Three Introductory Questions

1. What is abuse?

According to the Webster's Dictionary, abuse is "a deceitful act; deception; a corrupt practice or custom; improper use or treatment; physical maltreatment." In other words, any situation in which you have been lied to, mistreated, taken for granted, or overlooked is a form of abuse. When you are devalued in any situation, there is hurt and pain. The worst form of abuse is sexual abuse, but verbal abuse is also very painful. There are thousands of people who can scarcely function because of destructive words still lodged like arrows in their souls. Sexual abuse of women may include:

· Being forced to have sexual intercourse against their will.
· Being forced to allow the use of implements in intercourse.
· Being subjected to anal intercourse against their will.
· Being forced to dress up or perform acts which they consider to be degrading.
· Being forced to use or watch pornography.

Physical abuse can include a range of physical acts such as slapping, punching, thumping, burning, biting, kicking, shoving, choking, beating, shaking or "ragging," pushing someone down stairs and stabbing. However, women can be victims of physical domestic violence without ever actually being hit by their partner. There are many other forms of physical abuse that women have been subjected to, such as:

· Being put in a bath of cold water and scrubbed by the abuser until the skin bleeds.
· Being tied up.
· Having bags placed over their heads or being gagged.
· Having weapons held against them.
· Being made to sit absolutely motionless while the abuser spits at them.
· Being forced to use drugs.
· Having cigarettes stubbed out on them.

Unfortunately, as horrific as these physical acts are, they are only part of the story. Domestic violence also covers a range of other behavior that exerts power and control over the victim and amounts to emotional abuse.

Emotional abuse often causes the most damage. Physical violence may leave scars or bruising which will heal over time, even if it takes years. Emotional abuse, however, can leave deep but hidden wounds that can easily go without treatment, leaving the victims hurting for years to come. The after-effects of this type of abuse can change people's personalities and make it difficult for them to live a full life in the future without help and support.

2. Why do some Muslim men abuse their wives?

Why has Islam produced so much suffering for women despite the positive picture painted by Muslim apologists and feminists? Islam teaches that husbands are required to care for their wives; they have many duties related to them. But the Koran itself says that it is the duty of husbands to discipline and beat their wives if they persist in outright disobedience to their requests or orders.

> Men are in charge of women, because Allah hath made the one of them to excel the other, and because they spend of their property (for the support of women). So good women are the obedient, guarding in secret that which Allah hath guarded. As for those from whom ye fear rebellion, admonish them and banish them to beds apart, and scourge them. Then if they obey you, seek not a way against them. Lo! Allah is ever High Exalted, Great. (Sura 4:34, *The Meaning of the Glorious Koran*, Mohammed Marmaduke Pickthall, translator, London: George Allan and Unwin, Ltd., 1976)

This is a much-debated verse with a variety of interpretations. But what is obvious in this verse is that a progression of steps is to be used in dealing with a rebellious, refractory wife:
- The husband is to verbally admonish her.
- If that fails, the husband is to sexually desert the wife.
- If both measures above fail, the husband is commanded to physically beat his wife.

This Koranic verse has been used to assert male superiority and to justify abusive behavior. It explains why Muslim women are often victims of what can be described as "conjugal terrorism," which is economic, emotional and mental abuse, and which may lead to physical and sexual abuse. Conjugal terror-

ism includes verbal threats to divorce, remarry or take the children away if the
wife does not do exactly as she is told. It entails intimidation and threats of
harm; degradation, humiliation, insults, name-calling, ridicule, false accusations,
dismissal, neglect and a deluge of other forms. Conjugal terrorism can take
place in public or at home.

3. How does abuse in Muslim homes provide strategic ministry opportunities?

Many abused Muslim women do not seek help for several reasons:
- They are afraid of bringing shame upon their family if their situations
  become public.
- They are afraid of making their abusers more hostile.
- They lack confidence in themselves and believe that they somehow deserve
  the abuse.
- They depend financially on their husbands.
- They want to keep homes together for the sake of the children.
- They draw their identity and their sense of worth from their abusive hus-
  bands.
- They accept the abuse as a fact of life and learn to live with it.

However, if the Muslim victims of abuse decide to seek help within the
Muslim community, it is not easily found. If they turn to imams, they usually find
them unhelpful. Imams often tell these women to be patient and pray for the
abuse to end. Some imams make the abused Muslim women feel guilty, telling
them that they have brought the abuse upon themselves and instructing them
to go home and please their husbands. Other imams tell the women it is wrong
for them to discuss their problems with anyone other than their husbands.
Relatives are not a source of help either, as they normally encourage the
women to accept the abuse to avoid hurting the extended family's honor and
reputation.

In our ministry in Cape Town, we have noticed that abused Muslim women
often turn to non-Muslim women's organizations for help. They also find it easier to share their problems with non-Muslim women. Therefore, trained
Christian women who make the effort to befriend Muslim women get opportunities to introduce their Muslim friends to Jesus Christ, the Restorer of broken
vessels. Leading abused Muslim women to Christ is a relational process.

Restoring Broken Vessels

The following is a condensed version of the series of studies, "Restoring Broken Vessels." The overall objective of these studies is to encourage abused women to trust a loving God who cares and tends gently to those who come to him in need. Abuse demeans victims and takes away their choice and freedom, therefore it is important to listen and to allow discussions, interaction and reflection during the different sessions.

Taking an abused Muslim friend through the series "Restoring Broken Vessels" does not exclude the need for professional counseling. Jesus' message of healing and hope, coupled with professional counseling, helps the process of turning the abused person from a victim to a survivor.

It is important to help the abused person think through different solutions and face with her the practical implications of her decisions. It may be necessary to get a protection order from the court or put abused persons in safe houses or other places of safety. There have been instances of abused women having to live under South Africa's witness protection program because they were in danger.

Session I: Willing to Be Healed

Objectives:

- To listen to the victim and to plant seeds in her mind that will enable her to think through her own problems.
- To encourage the victim both to desire wholeness in her life and to trust and obey God.

God does care and He is able to sort out the messy realities of our lives because:

- God is compassionate (Psalm 103:8).
- God is forgiving (Ephesians 1:7; Romans 3:23-26).
- God is holy (Luke 1:49).
- God is immutable (Hebrew 13:8).
- God is just (Deuteronomy 32:4).
- God is loving (1John 4:16).
- God is omnipotent (Jeremiah 32:17).
- God is omnipresent (Jeremiah 23:23-24).
- God is omniscient (Psalm 139:2-4).
- God is righteous (Psalm 145:17).

- God is sovereign (Daniel 4:35).
- God is truthful (Titus 1:1-2).

He wants to help us discover ways of coping with our problems. But we need to want that help and have a willingness to change. God's methods of teaching us are gracious and gentle. He never bulldozes us. He waits for an invitation into our lives to help us with our problems.

<u>Passage to be studied:</u> John 5:1-9—The healing of the crippled man at the pool of Bethesda.

John informs us that among the multitude of sick people gathered around the pool was one "who had been an invalid for thirty-eight years."

Thirty-eight years! Think of that time span! Compare it with the length of your life. Think of all the events that have taken place during the past thirty-eight years.

Jesus chose this man out of the crowds and asked him what seems like a silly question: "Do you want to get well?"—"Do you want to be healed?" (RSV)

At first sight, it does sound rather obvious. Here is a man who has been ill for almost forty years and is lying at the side of a pool waiting and hoping for a cure. It is clear that he does want to be healed and get well. But is it? When Jesus asked the man if he wanted to get well, it was a valid and vital question. This probing question emphasizes the fact that what happens in us is more important than what happens to us. We are not able to choose what happens to us, but we can always choose what happens in us.

What went through the crippled man's mind when he heard that question? I have lost all hope of being healed. I don't deserve anything better. I am atoning for my past sins. I don't want to give up this life of settled and regular existence; after all, this shady setting by cool water is reasonably comfortable.

It is fascinating that the man did not answer Jesus' question. He should have answered with a simple "yes." Instead, he took the opportunity to complain and to blame others for his conditions. He had the mentality of a victim. Jesus cut short the sorry display of self-pity and gave him a command: "Get up! Pick up your mat and walk." Jesus asked the man to do what was literally impossible for him. When his will responded, his body was re-created, and his atrophied muscles were restored. The impossible was made possible. The Bible says that the right belief empowers. For the man at the pool, it was the right belief in the right person.

Do you wish to get well? Do you want to be healed? Do you really want to be made whole? What are your hesitations and your fears? What do you think is causing your emotional paralysis? Which areas of your life require healing? "Now to him who is able to do immeasurably more than all we ask or imagine, according to his power that is at work within us, to him be glory in the church and in Christ Jesus throughout all generations, for ever and ever! Amen" (Ephesians 3:20-21).

Session II: Jesus Christ the Healer of Broken Emotions

Objectives:

- To help the abuse victim understand the reality of God's sovereignty over all things.
- To encourage her to find healing in Jesus Christ.

We all have asked ourselves: "Why does God allow the tragedies of life?" There is no answer to that question because it is the wrong question. We must come to terms with the reality that life in a sinful world is not fair. And in this place of pain and hurt, God will bring to pass all his wise plans of love for us. In God's dealing with his children, no suffering is meaningless. "And we know that in all things God works for the good of those who love him, who have been called according to his purpose" (Romans 8:28). So what should be our reaction when facing suffering? It should be a big Y.E.S.

Y—ield to God's purposes and seek His wisdom.

E—liminate misconceptions about suffering.

S—urrender to a plan of action.

Being loved by God does not guarantee immunity, protection or intervention from harm. Not even Jesus was spared from suffering. He faced intense loneliness. He was abandoned by his closest friends, and even God. Have we suffered more?

Because of His suffering, Jesus can understand and feel our heartaches, our difficulties, and our failure. Who could be a better psychotherapist, friend and counselor than Jesus? Although Jesus may choose to work through human agencies, ultimately he is the healer of broken emotions.

Specifically, what can Jesus Christ do for those who hurt?

Passage to be studied: Isaiah 61:1-3—Jesus Christ the Physician of the soul.

This passage speaks of God's ability to deliver the Jews from captivity. And just as He liberated the Israelites, so he is ready to help us walk into freedom in the light of His love. "For I know the plans I have for you," declares the Lord, "plans to prosper you and not to harm you, plans to give you hope and a future" (Jeremiah 29:11).

Session III: Steps to Freedom and Wholeness

Objective:

· To give some practical steps which can start the abuse victim on the road to wholeness.

There is hope in the healing power of Jesus Christ. You can, like the man at the pool, stand up and walk and carry your mat (the symbol of helplessness) with you if you let Jesus Christ teach you to walk.

Eight steps you can follow that heal all your hurts:

1. Come into the presence of Jesus Christ.

In Acts 4:12 we read that there is salvation in no other name than Jesus. The word "salvation" comes from a Greek word meaning "to make whole." Jesus came not only to forgive sins but also to heal the sick and the hurts of the brokenhearted. Nothing is impossible with Jesus. And "Jesus Christ is the same yesterday and today and forever" (Hebrews 13:8).

2. Expose your wounds to Jesus.

Before any hurt can be healed, you must open it up to Jesus. To start the healing process as a victim of abuse, you must be willing to acknowledge eight truths:

· I have been abused.

· I am a victim of a crime against my body and soul.

· As a victim, I am not in any way responsible for the crime, no matter what I might have experienced or gained as a result of the abuse.

· Abuse has damaged my soul.

· The damage is due to the interweaving dynamics of powerlessness, betrayal, and ambivalence.

· My damage is different from others' in extent, intensity, and consequences, but it is worthy to be addressed and worked through no matter what occurred.

· It will take time to deal with the internal wounds; the process must not be hurried.

· I must not keep a veil of secrecy and shame over my life experience, but I am not required to share it with anyone I feel is untrustworthy or insensitive.

Next, get in touch with your true feelings. Sometimes it helps to write down how you feel and what hurt you. Be specific:

"I hurt because _____

_____."

3. Grieve your losses.

The first step in grieving involves acknowledging the loss. The second step requires you to realize your loss. The third step is to assess the damage.

To help you acknowledge that there is a loss, pause for a moment. Shut your eyes and ask God to reveal your losses to you. Ask God to remove the clutter in your mind so that you can see clearly what is affecting you. Try listing your losses (loss of love and support, loss of trust, loss of consistency and normal family life, loss of security, loss of material possessions, loss of affirmation and self-esteem.) Write them down on a piece of paper. Take the paper in your hand. Raise it up to the Lord and ask Him to heal that pain and that loss. Ask Him to give you peace as you surrender all these emotions to Him.

4. Confess your hurt as well as wrong attitudes.

True confession means you stop pointing the finger and playing the blame game. No matter how unjustly another person has wounded you, you must become responsible for your own attitude. If there is any trace of resentment, bitterness or hatred in you, you will not heal until you accept responsibility for it and confess it as being wrong.

This step helps you clean out your wounds.

5. Extend to the one who has hurt you the same forgiveness you have received from God.

"For if you forgive men when they sin against you, your heavenly Father will also forgive you. But if you do not forgive men their sins, your Father will not forgive your sins" (Matthew 6:14-15).

6. Thank Jesus because He is touching you with His love and healing power.

7. Relinquish your past hurt into Jesus' hand.

"Do not take revenge, my friends, but leave room for God's wrath, for it is written: 'It is mine to avenge; I will repay,' says the Lord" (Romans 12:19).

8. Take a positive action.

"Do not be overcome by evil, but overcome evil with good" (Romans 12:21).

"Being confident of this, that he who began a good work in you will carry it on to completion until the day of Christ Jesus" (Philippians 1:6).

Session IV: Two Tools for Healing:
A Positive Self-image and Forgiveness

Objectives:

· To show from the Scriptures how God is infinitely interested in us and how we are immeasurably loved by Him.

· To show how forgiveness plays a great part in the healing of the soul.

A Positive Self-image

When people have been deeply wounded, they often feel as if they have no self-worth, no value as human beings. Feelings or thoughts like these do not come from God. They have their origin in Satan, the father of lies, the accuser and the destroyer.

God affirmed our worth and value in the gift of Jesus Christ's death and resurrection (John 3:16-17). When we put our faith in the Lord, we are "in Christ." That is we have a new identity, which is based on a new relationship. The change is so radical that Jesus described it as being born a second time (John 3:3). Biblical truth is the cornerstone of our self-image, our self-esteem and our self-worth.

Study the chart on the next page to see who you are in Christ. (Used by permission, from Neil Anderson's book, *Living Free in Christ*, ©1993, Gospel Light/Regal Books, Ventura, CA 93003)

IN CHRIST

I AM ACCEPTED

John 1:12	I am God's child.
John 15:15	I am Christ's friend.
John 17:9.12.14	I am a gift to Jesus from God.
Romans 5:1	I have been justified.
1 Corinthians 6:17	I am united with the Lord, and I am one spirit with Him.
1 Corinthians 6:19,20	I have been bought with a price.
1 Corinthians 12:27	I am a member of Christ's body.
Ephesians 1:1	I am a saint.
Ephesians 1:5	I have been adopted as God's child.
Ephesians 2:18	I have direct access to God through the Holy Spirit.
Colossians 1: 14	I have been redeemed and forgiven of all my sins.
Colossians 2:10	I am complete in Christ.
1 Peter 2:9	I belong to God.

I AM SECURE

John 6:47	I have everlasting life.
John 10:10	I have abundant life.
John 17:9 - Hebrews 7:25	I am in Jesus' prayers.
Romans 8:1,2	I am free forever from condemnation.
Romans 8:28	I am assured that all things work together for good.
Romans 8:31f	I am free from any condemning charges against me.
Romans 8:35f	I cannot be separated from the love of God.
2 Corinthians 1:21,22	I have been established, anointed, and sealed by God.
Colossians 3:3	I am hidden with Christ in God.
Philippians 1:6	I am confident that the good work that God has begun in me will be perfected.
Philippians 3:20	I am a citizen of heaven.
2 Timothy 1:7	I have not been given a spirit of fear but of power, love, and a sound mind.
Hebrews 4:16	I can find grace and mercy in time of need.
1 John 5:18	I am born of God, and the evil one cannot touch me.

I AM SIGNIFICANT

Matthew 5:13,14	I am the salt and light of the earth.
John 15:1,5	I am a branch of the true vine, a channel of His life.
John 15:16	I have been chosen and appointed to bear fruit.
Acts 1:8	I am a personal witness of Christ's.
1 Corinthians 3:16 - 6:19	I am God's temple.
2 Corinthians 5: 17f	I am a minister of reconciliation for God.
2 Corinthians 6:1-1 Cor. 3:9	I am God's co-worker.
Ephesians 2:6	I am seated with Christ in the heavenly realm.
Ephesians 2:10	I am God's workmanship.
Ephesians 3:12	I may approach God with freedom and confidence.
Philippians 4:7	I have the peace of God, which transcends understanding.
Philippians 4:13	I can do all things through Christ who strengthens me.

Used by permission, Living Free in Christ, by Neil Anderson, ©1993, Regal Books.

Forgiveness

God is the great physician. He wants to heal you. But part of your healing depends upon your willingness to follow his prescription, and that is to forgive. <u>Passage to be studied</u>: Matthew 18:21-35—The parable of the unmerciful servant.

Some principles of forgiveness:

· Forgive quickly (verse 22).
· Forgive repeatedly (verse 22).
· Forgiveness is costly (verse 27).
· Forgiveness begets forgiveness (verse 33).

When you are unable to forgive, allow "Christ in you" to forgive through you (Galatians 2:20).

Someone in a physically abusive situation must forgive but may also need to get away from the abuser. Opening your heart to forgive does not mean closing your eyes to abuse. In the case of a physically abusive situation, forgiveness does not automatically necessitate immediate and limitless reconciliation as it may promote the abuser's sin. Giving the abuser opportunities to go on abusing would clearly violate the teaching of Ephesians 5:11, which tells Christians to "have nothing to do with the fruitless deeds of darkness, but rather expose them."

Action step

· **Begin a forgiveness list**—List your hurts, feelings and thoughts at the time of abuse and include a space to indicate the date when you chose to forgive. It is important to record the date when you chose to begin forgiving because you can refer to it when the inevitable emotional setbacks come.

Only God forgives perfectly. The rest of us have to keep working at it with continual recommitment to forgive when painful memories flood up.

Session V:—Restored for Potential and Purpose

Objective:

· To show that God has a purpose for the grief He brings or allows to come into our lives.

All of us experience adversity at different times and in varying degrees throughout our lives. In the arena of adversity, the Bible teaches us three essential truths about God:

- God is completely sovereign.
- God is infinite in wisdom.
- God is perfect in love.

God in his love always wills what is best for us. In his wisdom, he always knows what is best, and in his sovereignty he has the power to bring it about.

Passage to be studied: Romans 8:28-30

What is the good that God promises to bring about in our life? Conformity to the likeness of his Son is promised. God wants every believer to be like his Son. And he uses the painful trials and struggles of living in a sinful world to accomplish his purpose. He never wastes the pain of his children.

God's redemptive purpose can be served through the pain in our lives in a number of ways. Living through pain can help us develop godly character. It can also give us a way to glorify God, and it equips us to comfort and encourage others. Regardless of how dark the stains are in your life, God's creative potential is unlimited. He can take the very thing you view as most hideous and transform it into something that will make you most usable to him.

But it doesn't happen automatically; you must invite God into your life to do it. "For it is by grace you have been saved, through faith—and this not from yourselves, it is the gift of God—not by works, so that no one can boast. For we are God's workmanship, created in Christ Jesus to do good works, which God prepared in advance for us to do" (Ephesians 2:8-10).

These verses assure us that God's transforming power is part of a "package deal." God does not begin to make you his workmanship until you have become his child by receiving his gift of grace by faith.

- If you have never done that, would you do it now?
- If you have already acted on the truth of verses eight and nine, would you ask God to give you the faith to move into the truth of verse ten?
- Pray that God will remove the veil from your eyes and show you that he can redeem the seemingly destructive traumas of your life and use them for your good and his glory. Write out your prayer.

Steps of action

- Set specific spiritual goals for the future. List character qualities you want God to develop within you. Target specific areas of change in your personal disciplines and relationships with others.
- Make all the changes in your life you would make if you knew you had exactly one more year to live.

• Turn from every sinful act or attitude that God brings to your mind. Let such an affirmation become a part of your daily walk with God.

"Praise be to the God and Father of our Lord Jesus Christ, the Father of compassion and the God of all comfort, who comforts us in all our troubles, so that we can comfort those in any trouble with the comfort we ourselves have received from God" (2 Corinthians 1:3-4).

BIBLIOGRAPHY

Glaser, Ida and Napoleon John. *Partners or Prisoners? Christians Thinking about Women and Islam*. Carlisle, UK: Solway, 1998

Twombley, Kay. *Where Was God When I Cried?* Shippensburg, Pa: Destiny Image Publishers, 1998.

Poling, James Newton. *The Abuse of Power: A Theological Problem*. Nashville:Abingdon Press, 1991.

Seamands, David A. *Healing for Damaged Emotions: Recovering from the Memories That Cause Our Pain*. Colorado Springs: Chariot Victor Publishing, 1981.

Questions to Ponder

1. Why do you think the abused Muslim women of Cape Town respond positively to these studies intended for abused Christian women?
2. Based on these studies, what guidelines do you think can be followed to lead abused Muslim women in any culture to Christ?

Hasinoro Raja has been ministering among the Muslims of South Africa for the past eighteen years.

Ways to Reach Out to Muslim Women

Compiled by Jan Noonan

Introduction

Is it hard for you to reach Muslim women? Are you wondering how to spend more time with your Muslim friends or what to talk about with them? Here are some ideas compiled from a workshop to help you find ways to meet women. Also included are activities to do with women and conversation topics that may help spark a friendship. Please note that not all of these ideas are appropriate for every situation. You may need to evaluate your locale to decide which of these ideas will work for you.

We share these ideas based on three assumptions. The first is that the best way to learn culture and language well is to spend time with people. Second, our communication of the gospel becomes more relevant to people as we learn to live within their context. Finally, we gain our Muslim friends' confidence and trust in the context of friendship.

Scripture encourages us to reach out to Muslim women. John 17:15 promises that as we do, God will keep us from the evil one. Also, the Apostle Paul stated, " ...I make myself a slave to everyone, to win as many as possible" (1 Cor 9:19).

Perhaps the most important prerequisite for meeting Muslim women is prayer. Ask God to help you overcome any fears you have. Intercede for guidance and discernment regarding whom to approach, call or spend time with. Pray that God would bring into your life a local "woman of peace"—a woman of influence who is respected by the local Muslim women. Ask him to guide you to women with whom you have common ground. Finally, pray that our Father would guide you into meaningful contact with Muslim women, that he would use your life to speak the good news of the gospel.

We may encounter problems as we seek to reach out to Muslim women. Some of us may spend the bulk of our time at home with small children. Some may feel they don't have much in common with the women around them. Others may have a Muslim friend but are aware of the need to deepen the friendship. Still others may notice their friend never reciprocates, always taking but never giving. Finally some find that the women they want to meet are hidden away in the community. This article addresses some of these issues.

Where to meet women

Scripture includes many examples of where and how people were contacted. Jesus' followers met with people in many places, including a place of worship (Acts 17:23), a place of prayer (Acts 16:13), a synagogue and a market (Acts 17:17), at work (Acts 18:3), or at school (Acts 19:9). They were invited into homes (Acts 10:22) and even invited themselves into homes (Matt 10:11). Where do people meet in the course of normal life within your cultural context? Where do they socialize? Where do adults or children go to have fun?

The following is a list of potential places and activities that lead to contact with Muslim women:

- Neighborhoods
- Public transportation
- Schools
- Colleges
- Continuing education
- Education seminars
- Children's school or daycare
- Work
- Stores
- Government offices
- Public bathhouses
- Sports clubs
- Women's associations
- Public parks
- Beaches
- Amusement parks and attractions

- Tourist sites for locals
- Cafes and restaurants
- Concerts and special events
- Looking for housing
- Hiring help
- Buying services
- Running errands

The friendship established with a woman will extend into her network of relationships—her family and friends. Similarly, the relationships husbands and male teammates establish with men may open the door to relationships with their female family members.

In our interactions with women, we want to use words that reflect our roles as learners. We can communicate this by sharing: "I'm new here. I need to know ... I need to learn ... Where do I find ...? How do I ...? I need a friend. Can you help me?" We can explain that we are learning the language and need to practice with someone. We can ask for help communicating or translating. Our initial helplessness and our continued willingness to learn will open many doors. We can approach total strangers with questions like, "What time is it? Where's the bathroom? Can you direct me to ...?"

Activities that reflect that we are learners

As learners, we must be willing to be vulnerable, choosing activities that reflect our needs and our roles as learners of language and culture. A guiding question for us should be, "What are my children's/family's/my own needs that my Muslim friend can meet?" Some activities that present us as learners are the following:

Practice language.
- Ask questions about language or culture.
- Learn to cook food or drink.

Learn something new, such as knitting or another craft or skill.
- Ask logistical or personal advice.
- Live with a local family for a time in order to bond with them.
- Get a haircut. (The cut may be shorter than you planned, if the conversation gets going!)

Activities that are neutral

To participate in relationships with women as neither a learner nor a teacher, but a peer, you may want to ask other questions. What do women normally do together? When do women call each other? When do women visit each other? The following are "neutral" activities that bring you into contact with Muslim women:

- Look at pictures of family and friends; tell about your family.
- Watch television together; use it to bring up topics; or get used to ignoring the television and start conversations.
- Tell stories; this can easily lead into spiritual truths and the gospel.
- Go to places and do things listed above in the "Where to meet women" section.
- Walk through the neighborhood with your children during the time of day when others are out.
- Meet with other mothers for the kids to play together.
- Form a formal play group.
- Plan outings with women and children.
- Make phone calls on special occasions or just to say, "How are you?"
- Visit anytime or on special occasions when many are present.
- Visit when someone is sick to be supportive and pray.
- Accept an invitation to a "family home" for the weekend or a special event.
- [a] Attend a by-invitation event, for example, an engagement, wedding, birth ceremony, circumcision, funeral, feast or other party.
- Attend a Koranic reading or recitation.
- When pregnant, find other pregnant ladies and spend time together; join a prenatal class.
- Invite the families of your husband's soccer friends for a picnic together to meet the whole family.
- Go to a concert.

Activities that present you as a giver

Some activities present you as a teacher, as someone who meets needs. Ask God to show you the needs of the women you know and give you wisdom regarding how he wants you to meet those needs. Ask yourself, "What skills or knowledge do I have that I can share? What are the needs of women I know or want to know? Can I meet any of them? When do women give gifts?" The following are activities that focus on meeting the needs of others:

- Teach something—a craft or skill such as cooking, literacy, English or other foreign language.
- Offer to pray for your friend, provide a service or meet a need; for example, a nurse might administer shots to neighbors and their children.
- Give a gift, for example, food, small gifts, special occasion gifts.
- When there is a major celebration for a family, such as a birth, take a gift of sugar or rice and help with the preparations.
- Host a party on one of your special occasions—birthday or holiday.
- Start a group that meets occasionally or regularly that teaches something or meets a need, such as an English conversation group.
- Participate with your friend in community services, for example, a community "clean up" event.
- Hold a seminar on raising children.
- Start a women's tea house.
- Visit and offer condolences in crisis situations, such as the death of a family member.

Directing conversation to the Scriptures

The Bible can be brought into any conversation by saying, "I was reading in the Bible the other day about ..." or "Let me show you what I read in the Bible this morning." Contacts with Muslim women can be turned into opportunities by finding and memorizing Scripture that relates to natural conversation topics. Keeping in mind our roles as learners or givers, we can take the conversation to the Bible by bringing up verses relevant to the topics below:

- Your language learning process
- Circumstances in her life, school, work, home
- Circumstances of her family members
- Relationships among family members, friends, neighbors
- Interaction with government officials, employees
- Cultural learning questions
- Her practice and experience of religion or the spiritual realm

- Women's health topics: illnesses, treatments, preventative health measures, fertility, childbearing, breast-feeding, exercise, fitness
- Topics related to children: raising children, children's health, discipline of children
- Nutrition and eating habits, cooking
- Topics related to marriage: expectations, how she got married, characteristics of a good or bad marriage or wife
- Views of other women in her country: What are "most women" like? What defines "good" people and "bad" people?
- Views of money, financial topics
- Character traits in people (leading to fruits of the Spirit)
- Growing older, looking back at the past, planning for the future, death
- Current events (avoiding politics or being general and gracious regarding them)

This document is the result of a workshop presented at an international conference of overseas workers in August 2000. The original compilation is under copyright to Frontiers, PO Box 31177, Mesa, AZ 85275.

Compiled by Jan Noonan, a worker in North Africa.

PART THREE

Muslim Women and Muslim Background Believing Women

Why Muslim Women Come to Christ

by Dr. Miriam Adeney

"Mommy, why am I doing this?" Seven-year-old Habiba rubbed her bleary eyes with her knuckles. Half-asleep, hair tousled, nightgown rumpled, she could hardly stand up straight.

"We simply have to do it, little one," her mother answered, as she unrolled the prayer rugs. It was 3:00 a.m.

"If I'm praying, there should be somebody listening," Habiba murmured, struggling to consciousness. "He should answer. God should be like Daddy. When I talk to him, he answers. I respect God. I honor him. Why doesn't he talk to me?" At age six, little Habiba had been veiled. In her very orthodox Egyptian home, she prayed five times a day. Her mother was her mentor.

Yet in the bubbling, swirling maelstrom of Egypt, other influences flowed over Habiba. When she was ten, she spent a day with a friend. In the afternoon they went with her friend's mother to the dressmaker. Passing through the market, the mother paused. "Are those spices from ...? Wait here just a minute, girls." The mother ducked under the awning of the market stall, and for a few seconds the girls were free from supervision.

In that interval, a passing woman smiled at Habiba, and held out a small booklet. "Please take this book, daughter," the woman said softly. Startled and intrigued, Habiba received it. The woman floated on her way. What was the book? The girls puzzled out the title. *The Gospel of John*. Oh. A religious treatise. Worthy of respect, of course. But hardly interesting. When she got home, Habiba tucked the gospel into a drawer at the bottom of her dresser and forgot all about it.

The Word Brings Muslim Women to Him

As she grew, Habiba kept asking questions. Once in college, she studied philosophy more seriously. What was the basis of order in the world? How did the physical world hold together? What was the meaning of history? How could society be just? Habiba became a Communist sympathizer. From an orthodox Muslim to a Communist by way of philosophy—how could that be?

Egypt was bursting at the seams. Cairo's population had exploded. Sewage was inadequate. Transportation was inadequate. Basic postal, telephone, water and electrical services were inadequate. Housing was inadequate: two, three, or four families crowded into a small apartment, whether they knew each other or not. Health services were inadequate. Schools fell further and further behind in providing places for the children who needed to attend.

In the 1956 war with Israel over the Suez Canal, Egypt suffered great loss of reputation. In the 1973 war, Egypt lost more. In spite of a couple of great leaders, and in spite of trying several alternative political and economic strategies, conditions continued to deteriorate. What humiliation for the descendants of the pharaohs, the keepers of the Nile, the heirs of a great civilization.

Clearly a new approach was needed. Marxists at the university actively propounded one. Habiba even attended a course in Islam and Christianity taught by a Marxist professor. Marxism explained that workers should own the results of what they produced. Profits should not be skimmed off for absentee owners. A cooperative Marxist society would reward workers equitably.

So, longing for a healthy Egypt, longing for the justice that she studied abstractly in her philosophy courses, Habiba got caught up in the whirlwind of Marxism. She marched barefaced in the streets with the Marxists. But when each march was over, she put her veil back on, went home, knelt down, and said her prayers. Somehow, she thought, it all would *have* to fit together.

This was her life when, at age twenty-three, Habiba stumbled upon an outdoor Christian music concert on the outskirts of the university district. There were lutes and zithers, ancient psalms and new songs, haunting minor key melodies. Habiba was moved.

Before the concert, however, the lead musician prayed to "Father," and that confused Habiba. Who is his father? she wondered. The simple question nagged her like a sore tooth. Could he have been praying to God? But how does he dare to call God "Father"?

Then she remembered her 3:00 a.m. prayer times as a small child with her mother. She remembered protesting, "Why am I doing this? If I'm praying, there should be somebody listening. He should answer. If God is true, he should be somebody like my Daddy ..."Did these Christians really know God as a father?"

Back in her room that evening, Habiba was restless. Was it possible to know God more personally? Did the Creator actually care about relating to ordinary individuals in the chaos of Cairo? Suddenly she remembered the *Gospel of John* in her bottom drawer. She hadn't given it a thought for years. Of course by now she knew it was part of the Christian Scripture, the *Injeel*, the life of the Prophet Jesus.

Habiba crossed the room decisively, yanked open the drawer, and rummaged among the mementos and outgrown clothes. Was it still there? Hmm .. . No, that was her graduation program. How about this corner? Yes! She gazed at the little book, then crossed the room to curl up on the bed. She opened the gospel thoughtfully and began to read.

> *In the beginning was the Word ...*
> *Through him all things were made ...*
> *In him was life, and that life was the light of men ...*
> *He was in the world,*
> *and though the world was made through him,*
> *the world did not recognize him.*
> *He came to that which was his own,*
> *but his own did not receive him.*
> *Yet to all who received him ...*
> *he gave the right to become children of God ...*
> *The Word became flesh and lived for a while among us.*
> *We have seen his glory ...*
> *No one has ever seen God,*
> *but God the only Son who is at the Father's side,*
> *has made him known.*

Wow. The power of the poetry socked her. Blasphemy, probably. Son of God and so forth. True prophets don't get sidelined. "His own did not receive him?" And certainly the Eternal doesn't take on flesh. Still, what a radical concept. Appealing, too. The Creator visiting his planet in human form to show us his glory and share with us his power.

She read on. The stories were so human. A party, wedding, recorded in chapter two. She pictured the men dancing in their slow and stately way, the Prophet Jesus among them. Mary, a mother, calling on her son: "Pssst! We've got a little crisis here. They underestimated the supplies and the gatecrashers! Anything you can do to help?"

But then, in the cool garden under the stars, amid the fragrance of the night-blooming flowers, the Prophet Jesus advises the spiritual seeker Nicodemus, "You must be born again." What?

Nicodemus retorts—very sensibly—"How can a man be born when he is old? Surely he cannot enter a second time into his mother's womb?"

"No," Jesus answers, "Be born of the Spirit."

After painting word pictures of the Spirit, Jesus sets the "new birth" in context. "God so loved the world that he gave his one and only Son, that whoever believes in him should not perish but have eternal life ... [But, for those who ignore God] this is the verdict: Light has come into the world, but men loved darkness rather than light, because their deeds were evil."

Habiba found these words to be true: men did love darkness rather than light, even some Marxists and religious leaders. They twisted power in dark ways. What did it mean to "come to the light?" It apparently was connected with God's Son as an object of faith and with spiritual birth.

Habiba read on. In chapter four was a woman who had five husbands and now lived with another man! What was she, a nymphomaniac? Or had she been maltreated in a dysfunctional relationship and bounced onto a downward spiral? Habiba thought about women she had known who had been beaten, abandoned, or even raped. What were they to do? Especially if they had no relatives nearby. The Prophet Jesus treated this strange woman with amazing respect and took her theological opinions seriously. In the course of the discussion, he also claimed to be the Messiah.

Habiba continued reading. What compassion she saw in Jesus. What elegance in his philosophical arguments. Then she came to chapter eight.

> The teachers of the law and the Pharisees brought in a woman caught in adultery. They made her stand before the group and said to Jesus, "Teacher, this woman was caught in the act of adultery. In the Law Moses commanded us to stone such women. Now what do you say?"

They were using this question as a trap, in order to have a basis for accusing him. Suddenly Habiba's stomach began to churn. What could the Prophet Jesus say? Of course the woman had sinned. But where was the woman's partner? Did these bigots think she had been committing adultery with herself?

How unfair men were. And sometimes religious men were the worst.

Religion had sanctioned legal injustice and even brutality against women. She had seen it in her own community. It had disgusted her. It had pushed her toward Marxism or some other alternative. Now this beautiful gospel story would be ruined because of these hypocrites. The Prophet Jesus couldn't ignore adultery. In the end, he would have to agree to stoning the woman, wouldn't he?

Habiba closed the Bible with a snap, "I can't bear it. If he stones her, I don't want him. If he lets her go, I don't want him." She strode across the room and shoved the gospel back into the bottom drawer . "I don't want to read any more." She walked out and went to the lounge to watch television with the rest of the family.

But that night Habiba couldn't sleep. Finally she got up, crossed the room, and rummaged around in the drawer until once again she held the *Gospel of John* in her hands. She thumbed through the book. "What sura was I reading?" Ah, yes, chapter eight. Yes, here are the Pharisees. Here is the woman, dragged along. Here is their challenge. And here is the Prophet Jesus ... stooping down unconcernedly and writing with his finger in the sand, of all things.

> When they kept on questioning him, he straightened up and said to them, "If any one of you is without sin, let him be the first to throw a stone at her." Again he stooped down and wrote on the ground.
>
> At this, those who heard began to go away one at a time, the older ones first, until only Jesus was left with the woman still standing there. Jesus straightened up and asked her, "Woman, where are they? Has no one condemned you?"
>
> "No one, sir," she said.
>
> "Then neither do I condemn you," Jesus declared. "Go now and leave your life of sin."

Habiba sat quietly. "This is the Man for me," she said at last. That night she opened her heart to the Lord Jesus Christ as she had met him in the first eight chapters of the *Gospel of John*. She committed herself to Jesus as an object of faith. She asked to be born again through the Spirit. She asked for God's eternal life. She asked for the power to live in the light. Then, as an educated woman of Cairo, she went out and found a pastor to disciple her. For a year they met once a week.

Only then did she tell her parents. Very angry, they brought in a sheikh to deprogram her. Her pastor advised her to get theological training outside the country and then to come back. She went to Lebanon, where she lived with other believers from Muslim backgrounds and attended Bible school. In time, she met a believer from Europe who fell in love with her and married her. Today they minister to Muslims and whomever else the Lord brings. But the Man who will always matter most to Habiba is the beautiful Son of Man that she met in the *Gospel of John.*

There are many reasons why Muslim women come to Christian faith. One of the most powerful is the story of Jesus.[1] This story begins with the faith of a woman, Mary. It continues with the announcement of a prophetess, Anna. Jesus honored friends like Mary and Martha. He served women—the Samaritan at the well, Peter's mother-in-law, the adulteress, Jairus' daughter, the woman with a hemorrhage of blood, the widow of Nain, the Syrophonecian. Women were important at the cross and were the first to hear the news of Jesus' resurrection.

While some Jewish men thanked God that they were not born women, Jesus acknowledged their value. His stories sparkle with women who are capable of making choices—the lost coin, the widow's mite, the persistent widow, the wise and foolish brides, the woman using leaven, the queen of the South who will rise in judgement on this generation, and two women grinding grain together when the Lord returns.

Jesus came to show God to Muslim women. He came to conquer the powers of darkness that plague them. He came to reconcile them to God and others. He came to clean them from pollution, to serve as their sacrifice, to pay for their sins and to justify them before God. He has shown Muslim women how to rise above fate, how to suffer victoriously, how to nurture others and how to live focused on God. The story of Jesus is one of the biggest reasons Muslim women come to faith.

Other parts of Scripture—especially the narratives, poetry, proverbs, and prayers—attract women. These may be shared through many media. The JESUS film is available in almost 700 languages, including ten dialects of Arabic.[2] A ten-month curriculum of Bible stories for Arab women, carefully chosen for the breadth, balance and relevance of its themes, has been developed by a veteran missionary.[3] Indigenous Scripture songs and dances serve as wonderful teaching tools.

The value of Scripture memorization should not be underestimated. Muslim women come from a tradition of memorizing religious texts and usually begin doing so from a very young age. In Pakistan, a woman medic has seen 640 Muslims come to faith over a thirty-year period. New believers immediately begin memorizing 42 verses on salvation from the *Gospel of John*. With this limited resource, even an illiterate field laborer can become an effective evangelist. Through contests, literate younger people have been stimulated to memorize whole books of the Bible such as Ephesians, Colossians and Philippians. Out of this mostly-female body of believers, eleven boys have grown up to become pastors in the Pakistani church.[4]

Life Passions Bring Muslim Women to the Lord Jesus

Zaide heard God through one of the strangest stories in the Bible. Graduating with honors from the university, Zaide landed a job in national radio. She went on to do television ads and eventually became national marketing director for some large companies. She made a great deal of money. In her leisure hours, she was immersed in music, art, drama, books, clothes, dancing and entertainment. Active in the performing arts, she was a popular amateur singer.

A young man returned from the U.S. with an M.A. in theater. Soon he was head of a major theater group. Jorum was a handsome and talented dancer who knew all about music. He was also adventurous and outrageously flirtatious. Hungry for knowledge and experience, Zaide was instantly attracted to him. They began to date.

"Why won't you go all the way with me?" Jorum pressed her.

"Let's wait for marriage," she said.

"Ha! You put on a facade that you're so sophisticated but really, you're not," he taunted her.

So they had sex and she got pregnant. He sent her to a doctor to get an abortion. The doctor deliberately was incompetent. He gave her injection after injection, but nothing happened. Eventually, because of political pressure, Jorum married Zaide, but he did so reluctantly.

The marriage was not a happy one. Abuse began to rear its ugly head. And in the evenings Jorum would dress up and go out to night clubs without her. "Can't we spend some time together, Jorum?" Zaide would ask.

"I'm going out, and you're not coming with me," he would sneer. "If you want to go out and find your own fun, do it. But not with me."

One night Zaide sat on the steps in the backyard, gazed up at the stars, and clenched her fists. "I will avenge myself," she swore. Looking back, she says that is when she opened herself to evil.

In time, she fell in love with another, abandoned her husband and two children and moved in with her lover, Sharif, who was a very public figure. Zaide loved Sharif and believed he loved her. They had a daughter. But Sharif also had a wife with whom he continued to have children. In time Zaide began to realize how much she had lost.

Stresses spiraled. Zaide was robbed twice at knife point. Her car was demolished in a wreck, though she escaped unscathed. Several times she teetered on the brink of bankruptcy. Evil seemed to be stalking her. More troubling than these external problems, however, was her sense of personal sin. How she longed to be clean before God. Turning to religion, she started wearing the veil, praying five times a day and fasting. But her greatest desire was to experience forgiveness. She searched the Koran for a verse which would wash her clean from her life of sin, but the verses she read condemned her to hell.

Meanwhile, in spite of her domestic disaster, Zaide's career soared. Moving from one high-paying job to another, she had power over huge budgets. She had a nationally-recognized magazine column. She appeared on the radio and television. She drove the latest cars. Many people jumped to do her bidding. Nevertheless, she felt hollow. "I went through my days writing scripts and making money, but I was a shell," she says now.

That was her life when she encountered Bob, a fellow journalist whom she had known when they were both starting out years ago. His sense of peace impressed her. "Bob, what's happening in your life these days?" Zaide asked. "You look so relaxed."

"Well, to be honest, I'm involved in a Bible study group. And on the weekends I go to prisons. I talk to the drug addicts and other prisoners there. I get a lot of fulfillment out of that," he answered. Bob's background was not Muslim.

"A Bible study!" she exclaimed. "I haven't seen a Bible in thirty years. Not since school."

"I'll find you one," he said.

The next day, when she came into her office as usual, all her secretaries looked at her strangely. "Ma'am, a gentleman has left something on your desk," one said. There was a Bible. Of course the secretaries were thinking, "What's this Muslim woman doing with a Bible?"

But Zaide was touched by Bob's thoughtfulness. "How kind of him to remember our casual conversation and go to the trouble to bring me this book," she thought.

As it happened, it was the hour for prayer. Usually Zaide retired into her prayer room at this hour. Today she picked up the Bible and took it with her so that the secretaries wouldn't continue to be distracted. Placing the Bible on a side table, she prepared herself for ritualistic worship. She slipped on the white *telekung* which covered her entire body, leaving only her face bare, which she had wiped clean of any make-up. She rolled out the prayer mat and began.

But she could not focus on the recitations. The Bible nearby broke into her concentration. In a burst of impatience, she grabbed the Bible, thinking, "If there is a God, let Him speak now!" At random, she opened the book, and read immediately the words of Hosea.

> *Rebuke your mother, rebuke her,*
> > *for she is not my wife*
> > *and I am not her husband.*
> *Let her remove the adulterous look*
> > *from her face*
> > *and the unfaithfulness from between*
> > *her breasts.*
> *Otherwise I will strip her naked*
> > *and make her as bare as on the day*
> > > *she was born;*
> *I will make her like a desert,*
> > *turn her into a parched land,*
> > *and slay her with thirst.*
> *I will not show my love to her*
> > > *children,*
> > *because they are the children of*
> > > *adultery.*
> *Their mother has been unfaithful*
> > *and has conceived them in disgrace.*
> *She said, 'I will go after my lovers,*
> > *who give me my food and my water,*
> > *my wool and my linen, my oil and my drink'*
>
> —Hosea 2:2-5

Zaide's heart was pounding. "This is about me," she said, trembling. "My child was conceived like this. I abandoned my other children. I chased after a man. And I am a desert."

Hosea is the strange story of a godly man whose wife became a prostitute. He pursued her at God's direction and loved her back. They lived a metaphor of God and his people. God's people were faithless, but God went after them and loved them back. God's loving, forgiving faithfulness is what Zaide discovered when she read on. So many promises—

> *I will lead her into the desert*
> > *and speak tenderly to her.*
> *There I will give her back her vineyards*
> > *and will make the Valley of Achor a door of hope.*
> *There she will sing as in the days of her youth …*
>
> *I will betroth you to me forever.*
> > *I will betroth you in righteousness and justice,*
> > *in love and compassion.*
> *I will betroth you in faithfulness,*
> > *and you will acknowledge the Lord.*
> *"In that day I will respond,"*
> > *declares the Lord —*
> *"I will respond to the skies,*
> > *and they will respond to the earth;*
> *and the earth will respond to the grain,*
> > *the new wine and oil …*
> *"I will plant her for myself in the land;*
> > *I will show my love to the one I called 'Not my loved one.'*
> *"I will say to those called 'Not my people,'*
> > *'You are my people';*
> *and they will say, 'You are my God'"*

—Hosea 2:14b-15c, 19-23

Zaide was touched by the message of hope given to her in verse 15 and the promises of love, compassion, justice and faithfulness. She knelt down and sobbed. "No man ever gave me an oath like this," she said. And she came to the Lord Jesus Christ then and there.

That was ten years ago. Since then, Zaide has taken formal Bible courses. She lives a simple God-fearing life. Two of her children have believed and been baptized, although one has recanted because of political and social pressure.

For the past several years, Zaide has been teaching English as a second language to atheist Russian Jewish immigrants. Using the Bible as one of her texts, she joyfully introduces them to their father Abraham and to his descendants by faith.

Women in traditional Arab families seem to talk about sex quite a lot. After all, attracting and keeping a man's attention is the major road to success. Throughout the Muslim world, breeding and birthing are frequent and focal activities. So, whether the focus is attraction or the ability to bear sons, sex matters.

Because Muslim women are concerned with attracting the right man, beauty is an important issue. What is true beauty; maidenly beauty; matronly beauty? What is beauty if you are infertile?

Likewise, as sex usually leads to children, Muslim women (and men) grapple with the difficulties of raising their sons and daughters to be moral and godly people in the modern world. How do Muslim parents approach child discipline, moral training, healthcare and even prayer as they counter negative modern influences such as the distribution of condoms in schools and other secular attitudes concerning sex education. These are potential points of contact for sharing with Muslim friends. Rich answers can be found for them in Scripture which provides many texts for meditation and discussion.

God's attitude toward a woman's body is another bridge. In Islam, women are considered to be polluted. All bodily processes which secrete substances are unclean. Women menstruate, give birth, suckle infants and clean up children's messes. Menstruating women cannot pray because it is believed that God will not hear them. Yet every missed prayer and fast adds to a person's spiritual indebtedness, so women are always "behind" spiritually. Even though women may try to "make up" days of prayer and days of fasting, they never really catch up with what God requires.

Furthermore, in Islam women are passionate, not reasonable. Thus women ensnare men, incite men to lust and distract them from reason and righteousness. Women in Morocco often are called hbel shitan (rope of Satan). Naturally then, a woman's testimony is worth only half as much as a man's.

But Jesus reached out his hand to a woman who had been bleeding steadily for twelve years (Luke 8). What a breath of fresh air it is for a wounded Muslim woman to hear this.

The Search for Social Justice Brings
Muslim Women to the Lord Jesus

Ladan's father was an international Iranian banker and import-export broker fluent in French, Russian, Persian, Turkish and Arabic. Because of his high view of women, Ladan's father insisted that her two brothers respect her. He gave her a fine education culminating in a master's degree in England. He saw to it that she was happily married.

Ladan's mother was educated in French in a local convent school. She was known for her kindness, even to servants—ensuring that they had regular time off to visit their families and checking that they had good clothing and extra food to take with them. "Far too liberal," her neighbors scoffed. But Ladan remembers her mother was "like a saint," though she never talked about religion.

Ladan's parents were Muslims, but ethics tended to overshadow theology in their circles. People of their class and generation were cosmopolitan and broad-minded. It was their servants who transmitted the traditional heritage and it was from them that Ladan learned the basics of Islam.

For her university studies, Laden went to England. She lived in that cold, northern country for six years. Often she was lonely . Letters from home were too few. Here she began to make the Muslim faith her own. She had brought with her a translation of the Koran in the Farsi language. Now, for the first time, she read the scripture through. She tried to approach God the only way she knew, by praying and following the way of Islam. Over the next decade, Ladan would discover dozens of books on Islam written in the Farsi language and would read all that she could. Still, when she married and had children, Ladan wished she had something more to offer them. "I wanted to learn a bigger truth so I could give it to my children and it could be the foundation for their lives."

Instead, the Iranian revolution exploded. The traditional government of the Shah was ousted. In its place rose a strict, religious regime. To Ladan this was a tragedy. Her country had been on the brink of playing a significant role in the modern world. Now it slipped backward.

"After the Revolution, it would appear we had been hurt greatly," she says. "I was angry with God. I got involved politically, trying to stop Khomeini."

This was dangerous. Ladan's family decided that she and the children should move temporarily to the United States. Her husband would stay behind to see what developed. Many Iranian families were following this route, if they could afford it.

Yet even in the U.S. Ladan found herself drawn into politics. Elite Iranian exiles like herself gathered frequently to plot the overthrow of Khomenei and the future of Iran. She came home from these sessions weary from the scheming and political machinations.

Then she discovered Christian television. Here, particularly in The 700 Club, she encountered the Lord Jesus. In contrast to the political intrigue among her friends and fellow collaborators, in contrast to the gossip that made up her world, Jesus stood apart as a perfect person. "Jesus was such a good man that, if he had five daughters, he could have gotten them all married," she says. To find peace, she turned on the TV and reveled in Jesus.

One day the anchorman of *The 700 Club*, Ben Kinchelow, asked his viewing audience, "Would you like to know Jesus as your personal savior?"

"Would I?" Ladan asked herself. "I don't know what that means. But yes, of course I'd like to be as close to Jesus as possible."

Ben Kinchelow invited responsive members of the audience to pray the sinner's prayer. "Fold your hands," he instructed.

Ladan did.

"—bow your head, close your eyes—"

Ladan did.

"—and repeat after me, 'Lord Jesus, I admit that I'm a sinner. I need you to forgive me. I need you to clean me up, to transform me, to renew me through the power of your death and resurrection ...'"

Ladan prayed sincerely. Yet if someone had asked her after that if she was a Christian, she wouldn't have said yes. In fact, that is what happened. Some time after praying with Ben Kinchelow, Ladan was enjoying a beautiful afternoon in a city park. A woman sat down beside her. She turned out to be a homeless "bag lady" who carried her possessions with her. They fell into conversation.

"What's your religion?" the bag lady asked. "Aren't Iranians Muslim?"

"Oh, I've left that behind," Ladan answered. "I'd like to follow Christianity. But I don't know how to go about it."

"Do you have a Bible?"

"No."

"Well, I have one that I stole from a hotel," the bag lady announced. She reached down into her bag, fished out the Bible, and handed it to Ladan. "Here, you might as well have it."

When she got home, Ladan put the Bible by her bed. Every night for the next two years, she read the passages underlined in red—the words of Jesus—committing many verses to memory.

Then once again Ben Kinchelow reached into her life."Would you like to find a church near you?" he asked.That was a new thought to Ladan. She had never considered a church."If you want a church, and you don't know where to go, call this number and we will find you a church close by," Kinchelow continued.

"Do I want a church?" Ladan mused. "Well, if he could find me an Iranian church …But that could never be.So what do I have to lose? I'll give him a call."

Two days later *The 700 Club* returned her call with the addresses of two Iranian churches in her immediate vicinity.At last she found people with whom she could talk about Jesus. Surprising things began to happen in her daily life. When Ladan was baptized, for example, her craving for cigarettes evaporated. For ten years she had smoked ten cigarettes a day. Several times she had tried to quit.The day she was baptized, she returned home late, only to discover she was out of cigarettes and all the stores were closed.The next day she didn't light up until noon and then only out of habit."What happened to my craving?" she asked herself. Little by little her smoking disappeared totally, without effort on her part.

Prayer became power. "Because I know God can hear me, I feel like I have a lot of strength." Praying, she was delivered from worry about finances. Sure enough, she soon got a source of income. After she prayed about her daughter's lousy boyfriend, he dropped out of the picture.

"Mom, please don't pray for us," her children pleaded, only half joking.

"It's gotten to the point that my children are afraid of the power of my prayers," she chuckled.

Christian doctrines began to make more sense. Teaching on the Trinity had bothered her for a long time. If Christ is God, how was the earth sustained when Christ was on earth? She wondered.Yet, if Christ has done so much for me, how can I think he's anything but God? The analogy of water helped her. Water is in the ocean. Water is also in the faucet. One quantity of water is vast. One is specific and limited.Yet they can be from the same source of water, both parts of the whole.

Some of Ladan's efforts to share her faith with her husband over the international telephone lines have been humorous."Look, Massoud, if you have any trouble, talk to Jesus," she urged.

"What? Who? What agency is he in?"

Ladan revealed how she had experienced salvation in Jesus, and how she longed for Massoud to be saved.

"Saved?" he retorted."You're saved? From what? From me?"

"Oh, Massoud, cast out those bad thoughts. They're from the devil," Laden answered.

"What! Now I'm possessed?" he groaned.

With these communication mixups, Ladan is praying more than she is witnessing. She is looking forward to seeing Massoud face to face.

Meanwhile, she enjoys God. "To find Jesus is like someone who has never eaten anything sweet. When he does, he says, 'I've found it!' God is wealthy and generous. He's not jealous of us being happy. Just like I want my children to be happy, so God wants us to be."

Ladan prays for Iran. Her ethical, socially-conscious parents raised her not simply to care for her own needs but also for those of others. Today she does not simply pray for herself, nor for the needs of other individuals but also for the Iranian people as a whole. "Every night I pray a long time for Iran. I feel for the Iranian people because I know the suffering that I went through without God. I don't want my people to die without the Lord. I know we're bad people, hardhearted, lacking concern for others, superficial, and manipulative. But we have suffered a lot now … and the people of Iran are my people."

Ladan owns three pieces of land in Iran. A few years ago they were confiscated by the revolutionary government. Miraculously she regained title. When conditions change, she dreams of starting a low-cost Christian clinic on one of the locations. In the meantime, she plans a Bible cassette distribution program to spread the gospel in the rural areas.

For some women, it is not gender but justice that is the issue. A righteous community is the longing of their hearts. Such women set up associations to teach hygiene and literacy classes. They lobby for better marriage laws. And some are spiritual leaders. There are women in Saudi Arabia who "claim erudition in Koran and Hadith as a means of advancing feminist interests …Through their ability to refer to Koran and Hadith, they can engage in dialogue with conservative men, drawing on examples of independent women from the life of the Prophet as their models."[5] These women subscribe to total body covering, even of hands and feet, to legitimize their right to argue for greater opportunities in work and education.

Women in Hamas, a political party in Israel and the West bank, recently sat in a meeting "modestly attired in hijab, answered sura for sura the men's pronouncements about what was or was not proper Islamic behavior. The women had ...the authority of their dress but also their education."[6]

Women in Pakistan are learning to be leaders, even as they participate in very fundamentalist women's groups, "developing performance, social and leadership skills, experiences with diverse people and situations, and a growing awareness of their capabilities ...Majales (home meetings) have brought women both fundamentalism and freedom."[7]

Sufi leaders in Nigeria guide initiates through various levels of formulas, prayers and practices. They interpret doctrinal questions, teach songs of praise to the Prophet Muhammad and local Sufis, advise on legal matters and dispense herbal and Islamic medicine. One of them has written many books. They know Arabic and receive degrees of ordination in the Sufi system. While most of their followers are women, one of them has read "tafsir," exegeting the Koran, in the Emir's palace for the whole community during Ramadan. Although frowned upon elsewhere, another woman leads major community worship for both men and women.[8]

Christian women also have modeled leadership in the Muslim world. Palestinian sisters have done this since the time of Jesus. In the past two centuries, foreign missionary women have made some amazing journeys. In the 1880s, the gently-educated Lilyas Trotter went to Algeria to pour out the rest of her life. She witnessed to women and men, nurtured new believers, and wrote, illustrated and distributed Christian publications. As an artist, she decorated her manuscripts with sketches of the faces and flowers of the desert. She filled her journals with sunsets, rock formations, oases, questions and testimonies of men and women, and promises of God.[9] She traveled regularly deep into the desert, where she found spiritually hungry people. She cried with those who suffered and even with those who apostatized. She loved Algeria, its people, its cultures and its natural setting.

Five times early in this century, Mildred Cable and two single friends crossed the Gobi Desert. They brought the gospel to Chinese Muslims who lived in an area beyond the Great Wall that was thick with bandits. They were kidnapped by a famous brigand. Through their efforts, people believed in Christ. Congregations were formed. Today even secular feminists are rediscovering and promoting this brave explorer's books.[10]

Maude Cary was one of the very few missionaries to stick it out in Morocco all through World War II. She was still opening new mission stations at the age of 72 and, when a Bible school finally was begun, half the students were fresh believers from her newest station.[11]

Long before there were antibiotics, jet travel and diplomatic immunity, women missionaries and local Bible women have traversed jungles and deserts and mountain ranges to bring good news to women inside the walls of harems and purdah rooms.[12] Like Ladan, they cared enough to dare.

Muslim women aflame for just and righteous communities may constitute an unreached people. No Christians have focused on them, to my knowledge. Yet we share a common longing—"Let justice roll on like a river, and righteousness like a never-failing stream" (Amos 5:24).

Dreams, Visions, Healing, and Exorcisms Bring Muslim Women to the Lord Jesus

Born in northern Iran, Simin was the oldest of three girls. Because her father had no sons, he tutored his daughters with great care. From an early age, Simin had a hunger for God.

One day when Simin was four, she heard screaming. Up the stairs she clambered, across her roof, and on to the adjoining roof, and the next, and the next, and the next. Finally she looked down to see what was causing the noise. In the courtyard below, she saw a dead baby. A woman was washing it. As she poured the water, she howled. Eventually a group of people carried the baby out of the yard. Simin followed, creeping along behind. Their destination was a cemetery. Because the Iranians don't use coffins, Simin saw them put the baby in a hole in the ground.

Running home, she begged her grandmother, "Why do they take human beings and put them in a hole in the ground?"

"Because people die. Where have you ..." began her grandmother.

"Why do they die?" Simin interrupted.

"Fate. When it's their fate, when it's their time, they have to go. We all have to ..."

"When they die, where do they go?"

"Ah, there's the mystery," the old woman's eyes narrowed. "They say there is a bridge ten thousand times finer than human hair. If you are good enough, you will be able to cross it when you die. Then you'll be in paradise. Food, music, pets, friends, luxury. Ah, but you, with all your naughtiness, you're more likely to end up in hell-fire, pain, screams of agony. You'd better watch out, pay attention, obey, be a better girl, shape up!"

Hell. Simin began to have nightmares. A few months later, soldiers came to the village to conscript young men. There was a knock at the door.

"Salaam Aleikum, Madam," the soldiers greeted Simin's grandmother."Peace be with you. It is our duty to inform you that we have a notice of conscription for two young men in your family, Ali Razak and Hussein ..."

Simin fled out the back door. Regardless of what they said, she knew that they were demons, sent to drag her to hell! All day Simin hid out behind a wall. All day she prayed, "God, I'll do whatever you want, just don't take me to hell. Don't turn me into a demon." Toward evening, she went down to the river to wash her hands and face. There she saw a man on the water.

"What are you doing here?" the man asked her.

"Washing my hands," Simin answered.

"Why don't you do that at home?"

Simin explained why she was afraid.

"What are you worried about?" the man smiled. "I am the one who decides who goes to heaven and who goes to hell. And you are going to be with me."

Peace flowed over little Simin. She wanted to hug the man. But she couldn't walk on the water to him. Instead, thoughtfully, she went home. For years Simin treasured that memory. How different this glimpse of the supernatural seemed from her grandmother's. Years later she would continue to hunger for God, sometimes impetuously and almost blasphemously. Not for religion. Not for a set of standards to keep. But for the God who made her, the God who knew her, the God who kept pursuing her, even as she pursued Him. Fourteen years after her conversion to the Lord Jesus Christ, when asked her favorite verse, Simin would say quietly and firmly, "The promise of God in Jeremiah 29:13: 'You will seek me and find me when you seek me with all your heart.'" Her story witnesses eloquently to the truth of that verse.

After Simin graduated from high school, she enrolled in nurses' training. She was a top student. But Iranian nurses who had graduated from British schools looked down on her. "Iranian nurse training? Very second rate," they mocked.

"Look, we perform many of the functions that doctors do in other countries," Simin and her friends protested.

"All the more fools, you. You perform the functions, but you lack the background theory. You diagnose by symptom, rather than understanding the comprehensive etiology ..."

This bothered Simin. One night, outside the nursing students' quarters, she prayed impulsively, "Lord, I want to get out of this country; I want to study overseas."

In record-breaking time she found herself in the United States. But she soon was homesick. One afternoon she took a dictionary and strolled aimlessly down the streets. She stopped in front of an attractive big building and read "church" on the sign in front. "Church?" she wondered, and riffled through the pages of her dictionary. "A place of Christian worship," she read. The soaring stone arches drew her with their hints of spaciousness and serenity.

"Well, now I'm in this country, and I need all the help I can get," she thought to herself. So she pushed open the thick oak door of the church and slipped in. She tiptoed down the aisle. The quiet, the stained-glass windows, the dust motes dancing in shafts of sunlight, the warm wood of carved pews—Simin was touched. She walked softly to the front and knelt down. Peace washed over her. Suddenly, as she began to unwind from the stresses of culture shock that had piled up inside her, she started to cry.

In time an old man came and knelt beside her. He talked comfortingly. He prayed. Simin hardly could understand a word. Just enough to give him her address when he asked. After that, he invited her to his home for dinner. He took her to church. And he dropped in for a visit at her apartment almost every day. While there he would read from the Bible. Again Simin couldn't understand. "What's he saying?" she would ask her roommate, who had been in the United States longer.

"He's trying to convert us," her roommate would sneer.

"Well, let him come," Simin answered. "No fear. We won't get converted."

So, day after day, the doorbell would ring. "Oh no, here he is again!" her roommate would groan, squinting through the peephole in the door. But Simin recognized the old man's warmth and love.

After a few months on the East Coast, Simin moved to the Midwest where she took a job as a nurse's aid in a convalescent home. One of her charges was an old lady. Simin washed and brushed her hair with care and dressed her attractively. The woman's daughter, a Catholic, appreciated Simin's thoughtfulness.

"Do you know Jesus, Simin?" the daughter asked one day.

"No. Only as a prophet," Simin answered. No more was said on the subject. But Simin remained aware that the old woman's daughter always looked at her with eyes full of love and concern.

Again Simin moved, this time to California, where she enrolled in college. However, life in America had begun to disillusion her. Neither her Iranian nor her American friends seemed to have much meaning in their lives. She began to spend more time alone. She would go out into the hills around Ventura and talk to God. "I see people turning into animals. No one is searching for you," she told God.

A brief visit home provided little help. Her family didn't know what to make of this American Simin. She walked differently, and she talked differently. She smoked two packs of cigarettes a day. As for Simin, "After two days," she recounts, "Iran was the same as America." She saw social patterns without significance.

Her mother called her to pray with the family at one of the regular daily prayers. But tradition was no longer enough for Simin. She wanted an authentic personal encounter with God. "I'm not going to kneel down unless God confronts me personally," Simin lashed out. "I've been kneeling down too long without knowing why."

Drawing her into the next room, her mother protested, "You don't have to raise your voice in front of your brothers and sisters. Don't rattle their faith, at least."

"Why not?" Simin retorted. "They need help, too. Where is God? What has our faith really done for us? How has it helped us to understand life better?"

If orthodox Islam seemed vague, the neighbors' Ouija board parties didn't offer anything better. Although these well-meaning friends urged her to join them for some sociability, Simin refused. "There has to be a Creator in charge, not just dead souls giving messages helter-skelter," she insisted.

After her visit home, she returned to California. Her hunger for God continued. She began asking people, even people she had just met coming out of a supermarket or a bank, "Can I ask you a question? Do you believe in God?" She started making a religious survey of her fellow students. She didn't find one "born-again" person. "All of me was a question mark," she recounts.

One day in anatomy class, she was dissecting a cat. Her partner was an Iranian man. Both were excellent students. In this exercise, one was supposed to read the instructions while the other performed the operation. But today all she could think of was the cat's Creator. "Who made you?" she kept asking the cat. She and her partner got sidetracked, discussing life.

When the professor came around to observe their work, he scratched his head and said, "I can't give you a good grade because everybody else is in the abdominal cavity and you're still on the superficial muscles."

Simin's partner was upset. He went to the professor. "May I talk to you privately, Sir? I think Simin is suicidal. That's why we didn't get much dissection done."

The professor called her in for a consultation and Simin unloaded. Why didn't anybody else demand significance from life? "The whole world is full of animals that don't know where they've come from and where they're going!" she exclaimed.

"You're wasting your time," the professor soothed her. "There is no God. Evolution has produced us. So enjoy. You're a young girl. Life is before you."

"Even a blind person knows there's a God," Simin retorted. "But I want to communicate with him. I've been talking. He hasn't been answering. I want to meet him face to face. There are some things I want to discuss with him."

A short time later the professor asked her to help him dissect a human cadaver. "How old do you think this man was?" the professor asked her as they began.

"Oh, quite old," she said, noting the many signs of aging.

"He was ninety-three."

"Ninety-three years old!" Simin exclaimed. She said to herself, "What gave him the power to go on that long? Did he know God?"

When the cadaver was opened, Simin saw the glory of God. "Lord," she breathed, "I see your signature over the liver, over the stomach. The wrist section is like guitar strings. You're beautiful, Creator. But can a human being know you?"

During this period, Simin wrote God a letter.

> *Do you remember when I was talking to you in my anatomy class?*
> *I'm from Iran. I'm a young girl. Everybody thinks I have so much.*
> *But I don't have anything, because I don't have You.*
> *God, I'm tired of running my life. Would you make friends with*
> *fools? If you would, here is one. I'm very lonely. All the things that*
> *other people on earth enjoy don't do anything for me. But I confess*
> *I'm nothing but trouble for you ...*
> *I don't know what mailman to give this letter to. Yet if you're pow-*
> *erful enough to create the cadaver, you're powerful enough to see*
> *me writing this letter.*
> *I don't know what to call you. Some call you energy. Some Allah.*
> *Some Buddha. You tell me who you are. I know you must have a*
> *personality.*

Simin thanked God three times in the letter. When she put down the pen, the Spirit of God seemed to come around her and hug her, and she received confidence that her letter would be answered.

But one night in her bathtub, feeling dejected and almost suicidal, Simin began crying. "God, either you take my life and do something with it, or let me take it," she said. A big wind rushed into her bathroom. It filled her being. Simin bowed over with sudden consciousness of her sin, of her unworthiness to negotiate with the Creator of the universe. "Oh yes, you're beautiful, you're majestic," she breathed, "but you're also a person before whom we have to fall flat on our faces."

"Congratulations!" God seemed to say to her. "You have been born again!" Very much like the French philosopher/mathematician, Blaise Pascal, when he recorded his climactic experience of God in 1654, Simin was flooded with joy. From 2:30 in the afternoon throughout the whole night, bliss and confidence washed over her. She didn't dare sleep. She didn't want to miss a minute of the enjoyment of God's presence.

In the morning her doorbell rang. "Hello. The Lord Jesus loves you," smiled the woman at Simin's door. She handed Simin a leaflet. Startled, glancing through it, Simin read, "Here I am! I stand at the door and knock. If anyone hears my voice and opens the door, I will go in and eat with him, and he with me" (Rev. 3:20).

"Who said this?" Simin asked.

"Jesus Christ," the woman answered.

"No! No! No!" Simin shouted inside. "I'm never going to give up the Muslim religion. If this is what you wanted to show me, God, I shouldn't have started looking for you. This is like asking me to take off my clothes and run across the grass naked."

Surely the God who had met Simin so sweetly couldn't intend this. Surely her visitor was misguided. Out of pity for the woman, wanting to help even Christians come to a true experience of God such as she now had, Simin agreed to go to church with her visitor.

After she had shared her experience with some of the people at church, the pastor quietly invited her, "Simin, would you like to be born again?"

"I am born again!" she exploded. "Didn't you hear what I said?"

"But do you follow Jesus? There is no other way to be born again except through Jesus. He is the way, the truth and the life."

"No, Jesus is only a prophet as far as I know. And as for you, you people ought to fall down in awe and reverence and worship God, not a man."

Although this exchange was stalemated, the worship service continued. Soon they reached the point in the service when most of the congregation went forward and knelt down for prayer. Simin did too. Falling on her knees, she prayed that these church people would have the joy of being born again that she had.

Some people's prayers were audible to Simin. They were speaking languages that weren't English. One lady said, "Tavakol beh Masih," which in the Persian language means "Trust in the Messiah."

When Simin raised her head, she was enraged to see that all around her Christians were praying for her, stretching out their hands toward her, though at a distance. As soon as the service was over, Simin went to the woman who had said, "Tavakol beh Masih."

"Do you speak Persian? Have you lived in Iran?" Simin asked her.

The woman seemed dumbstruck. Her husband nudged her. "Honey, you speak Persian!"

"Oh, I do?" the woman wondered.

"No, we've never been to Iran," the man explained to Simin. These are heavenly languages we're speaking. The Holy Spirit gives them to us. We don't always understand what they mean."

What kind of crazy people are these, Simin thought, that they don't even know what languages they speak! She made her exit as quickly as she could.

A woman ran after her down the sidewalk, calling, "Lady! Lady!"

Simin turned. "Yes?"

"Take this," panted the woman, holding out a Bible. While Simin hesitated, the woman began to explain the basic divisions, the Old Testament and New Testament. Seeing other people streaming out of the church toward her, and not wanting to get further entangled, Simin took the Bible quickly, muttered her thanks and got out of there.

All night long, until 8:00 the next morning, Simin read the New Testament, not even changing position in her chair. A small voice spoke to her about the Trinity, God the Father, God the Son and God the Holy Spirit. Simin got angry. "I don't want Jesus and I don't want the Holy Spirit. I just want you!" she begged.

She kept on reading the Bible, but she didn't go back to church. About ten days later, a general bulletin from the church landed in her mailbox. It included a questionnaire for new visitors, and a brochure. On the brochure an artist had drawn a loaf of bread and a stalk of wheat. Underneath were the words, "I am the bread of life."

"Truly, God, you *are* the bread of life, our necessity, our nourishment. But why is Jesus claiming this?" Simin murmured. Scanning the questionnaire, she decided, "I'd better let these church people know that there's no way I'm going to become a Christian." So she filled in the blanks with negatives.

"Are you interested in learning more about the Christian life?"

"No!"

"Are you interested in praying to receive Christ into your life?"

"No!"

Finished with that, she wrote a letter telling her father how stupid American Christians are, worshiping a man instead of God. Then she scooted across the bed in order to get up, go out and mail the two letters. As she reached the edge of the bed, suddenly she envisioned a pair of bare feet coming toward her. Then she saw the lower part of a garment above the feet. The cloth had a Jewish patterned figure, such as she had seen when she had done public health nursing in a Jewish community in Iran. The vision put its left hand on her face and said, "Go to sleep. The Lord is with you."

Drowsiness overcame her. She fell back on the bed and slept sweetly until morning. Then, as she woke, bits of the vision came back. "God, who was that Jewish man in my room last night?" she asked sleepily.

"The Lord Jesus Christ. The Lord Jesus Christ. The Lord Jesus Christ." Voices murmured it over and over. Unearthly music swelled.

Simin fell flat on her face. "Oh, Lord Jesus, forgive me," she cried. "I don't know if you know my background. I'm from Iran. I'm a Muslim. It's so hard for us to think of you as God."

Going back to the church, Simin asked for the microphone and told her story. That was twenty years ago. Since then, God has brought many beautiful Christian friends into her life. Still, it hasn't been easy. The first four years of her Christian life were constant fighting, Simin recalled. "God loved me, but he didn't like much about me." Nor was she quick to yield to him.

When she told her family of her conversion, her father said, "No Americans can change my daughter. The children that I brought up are rooted in truth." He asked the American embassy to deport her. Imagine his surprise when they told him they couldn't do that, since people have freedom of religion in America.

" Now when I see Iranians, I cry for them," Simin admits. Quite a few Iranians in the United States have come to know the Lord Jesus through her witness. People trust her, she says, because although she is blunt, she is kind and will not gossip. She has served as an elder in the two thousand member New Jerusalem Church in southern California. In addition to demonstrating a gift in evangelism, she also is known for a special gift in healing.

Jesus' Women

We are called to be khalifa who care for God's world, like Eve.[13] Yet many women in every culture forfeit this birthright, due to ignorance, selfishness, fear, or externally-imposed limits. What a waste of human resources. What potential lies undeveloped.

Jesus' women can live differently. They can live as though Saudi Arabia is the Lord's—Bangladesh is the Lord's—the markets and universities and multinational corporations are the Lord's. Jesus' women can be channels of God's love to the crowded cities, the transient guest workers, the broken marriages, the confused children, the atheist young adults, the government leaders scrambling for moral guidance. Jesus' women can show the beauty of righteousness, the wonder of grace, the power of godliness.

How the Muslim world needs the vitality of Spirit-filled young mothers! How the Muslim world needs a praying network of contented older women, role models with lifetime testimonies to the grace of God! How the Muslim world needs the challenging example of chaste and passionately caring single women!

Today the energies of Muslim women often are squandered. Few know that they are created in the image of God, redeemed by Christ, capable of being empowered by the Spirit, and called to active service in God's world. So old women gossip. Young women experiment with cosmetics and intrigues. Yet who knows how many human needs could be met if God through Jesus Christ would dynamize such women?

FOOTNOTES

The case studies in this paper are used by permission of InterVarsity Press. *Daughters of Islam* by Miriam Adeney, is available from InterVarsity Press. To order, please contact: mail@ivpress.com.

1.   There are all sorts of reasons why Muslim women come to the Lord Jesus Christ. Some come when they read the gospel story. Others come because they see Jesus in visions or dreams. Others, during a struggle with demons or spirits, find that the name of Jesus brings liberation and help.

Some come from abusive, dysfunctional relationships. Others have been schooled in the ideals of righteousness and long for justice in their societies. They find the power for this in the Lord Jesus. Some come because of Christ's affirmation of women. Some who have lived promiscuously cry out for a moral foundation for their own lives. Others fear death, and long for assurance of paradise. Two women whom I interviewed have hungered almost single-mindedly for God from their earliest childhood. Many come because their family has decided jointly to follow the Lord Jesus.

Who are Muslim women? Clearly they differ according to their national or ethnic identity. Beyond national ties, a woman's concerns also are shaped by her role in the life cycle, her economic situation, her ideological community and her personality.

Economically, some of the richest countries in the world are Arab. Yet there are many malnourished women among the Muslims of South Asia. Economically, some Muslim women have doctorates, while others are illiterate. Many Muslim women know little about Islamic doctrines and theology. They resort to folk religion, shrines, sacrifices, amulets, divination and spirit possession as often as they turn to Muslim institutions. Others are well-grounded in the teachings of the faith. For still others, political activism is what counts, rather than religious fervor. Even in a simple village, some women may specialize as herbalists, while others are textile weavers, food dryers, cheese makers, perfumer, Koranic reciters, musicians, occult women and land speculators.

Finally, each woman has a distinct personality, and distinct life experiences and opportunities.

2.   For information on the JESUS video, consult www.frontiers.org. or 1-800-462-8436.

3.   A.H., "Discipleship of Muslim Background Believers through Chronological Bible Storying," *Ministry to Muslim Women: Longing to Call Them Sisters.* Fran Love and Jeleta Eckheart, eds. Pasadena CA: William Carey Library, 2000.

4.   For supplemental discussion of this woman's ministry, see Iliam, "What Helps Muslim Women Grow in Christ," Ibid.

5.   Eleanor Abdella Doumato, "Women and Work in Saudi Arabia: How Flexible Are Islamic Margins?" *Middle East Journal*, 1999, p. 576.

6.   Elizabeth Fernea, "The Challenges for Middle Eastern Women in the 21st Century," *Middle East Journal*, Spring 2000, p. 190.

7.   Mary Elaine Hegland, "The Power Paradox in Muslim Women's Majales: North-West Pakistani Mourning Rituals as Sites of Contestation over Religious Politics, Ethnicity, and Gender," *Signs: Journal of Women in Culture*

and Society, 1998, pp. 391-423.

8. Alaine Hutson, "The Development of Women's Authority in the Kano Tijaniyya, 1894-1963," *Africa Today*, Summer-Fall 1999, pp.43-64.

    Wali Sulayman (1890-1939) was a northern Nigerian who encouraged women as Sufi leaders. He was surrounded by four spiritually thirsty women—his mother, sister, wife, and his Emir's wife—all of whom took advantage of every opportunity to learn. Wali Sulayman's wife taught in the Emir's household, handling classes of 100 boys at a time. For many of the current titleholders in the Kano Emirate, she was their first teacher. After her husband's death, she taught Koran, Arabic grammar, fiqh (Islamic jurisprudence), hadith (sayings of the Prophet), and tafsir (exegesis) at the Kano Women Teachers' Training Centres.

9. *Patricia St.John, Until the Day Breaks: The Life and Work of Lilias Trotter.* Carlisle UK: OM Publishing, 1990.

10. Mildred Cable, *The Gobi Desert*. London: Hodder and Stoughton.

11. *Ruth Tucker, "Maud Cary," From Jerusalem to Irian Jaya: A Biographical History of Christian Mission.* Grand Rapids: Zondervan Publishing Company, 1983.

12. See Dana Robert, "Revisioning the Women's Missionary Movement," in ed. Charles Van Engen, et.al., *The Good News of the Kingdom*. Maryknoll NY: Orbis Books, 1993; Dana Robert, *American Women in Mission: A Social History of Their Thought and Practice*. Machine, GA: Mercer University Press, 1996; Judith MacLeod, *Woman's Union Missionary Society: The Story of a Continuing Mission*. Upper Darby PA: Interserve, 1999; and Guli Francis-Dehqani, "CMS Women Missionaries in Persia: Perceptions of Muslim Women and Islam, 1884-1934," in eds. Kevin Ward and Brian Stanley, *The Church Mission Society and World Christianity*. Grand Rapids: Eerdmans' Publishing Company, 1999, pp.91-119.

13. Badru Katerrega and David Shenk, *Islam and Christianity: A Muslim and a Christian in Dialogue*. Nairobi: Uzima Press Ltd., 1980.

Words and Ways to Bless

Scripture, spiritual power encounters, and loving friendships: these are probably the three main ways that Muslim women are drawn to the Lord Jesus.

Beauty, sex and social justice issues are the paths for some women. But there are many more ways to build bridges.

- Visiting
- Prayer
- Song
- Rituals
- Thanksgiving services
- Books, videos, cassettes, storytelling, proverbs
- Health care, ESL, Microenterprise development
- Sewing or craft groups
- Classes in aerobics, parenting, beauty, fashion, history and culture, gardening, conflict resolution

More specifically, topics such as the following can be springboards for talking about the Lord Jesus. For example:

- Jesus' story
- Earthy biblical symbols—bread, water
- Women in Scripture
- Psalms, Proverbs, parables, Bible narrative
- God's names, Jesus' names
- Women of history and today
- Charms
- Veil
- Fasting
- Creed
- Submission
- Dreams
- Sacrifice feasts, especially Abraham's
- Fulfilled singleness
- Porno videos: What Christians think about sex
- Child raising
- Family planning
- Solving family conflicts
- Community social ethics
- God's creation, ecology
- Cultures: God-given creativity & sinful exploitation
- Repentance for Western sins
- Christ versus Christians

- Forgiveness
- Confidence
- Love
- Release from anger
- Power to do right

Dr. Miriam Adeney is the Associate Professor of Cross Cultural Ministries at Seattle Pacific University. Miriam is an anthropologist who has done extensive research of case studies of women believers in Jesus from Muslim backgrounds and has written a book on her findings entitled, Daughters of Islam, InterVarsity Press.

A Muslim Woman's View of God

by Ilaim

Asha Waits for Allah to Reveal Himself

Asha squatted under a dirty white sheet in a dark corner. The smell of henna-saturated mustard seed oil and rose water hung on the fetid air of her parent's adobe, mud-roofed room. Unwashed dirty bodies added a pungency all their own as groups of women came to sit with the bride-to-be. She herself added to the nauseating odor. Custom dictates that for ten days she could neither bathe, comb and oil her hair or clean her teeth. Each woman would rub her own face with the mustard seed oil mixed with flour and then rub Asha's arms, neck and legs. Then each washed herself with rose water to complete the beauty treatment.

Asha's heart pounded in fear as she thought about her fast-approaching marriage to an unknown older man. Allah was the creator of the world and all that it contained—sun, moon, stars, animals large and small, and both men and women. "Did Allah then abandon what he had made, separating himself like an absentee landlord?" she wondered.

Taunted by the older women with threats of cruelty in her future marriage, she was told that women were only created for the satisfaction and pleasure of men. "Did Allah truly not care for women? Was there no hope of happiness available to her?" she questioned. Allah seemed so impersonal and uninterested in her problems, fears, needs and cares. He seemed so very far away to her and to the other women with whom she dared to discuss her feelings.

"What about prayers?" she mused. The words were in Arabic which she did not understand. Prayers were to be said at mandated times—so stiff and formal. No matter. Allah was too busy or uninterested to hear and answer these daily types of needs and requests. Asha moaned, thinking that now it was too late to ask for a kind husband. Fear seemed to swallow her up.

Asha reached for her *tusba*, the three-sectioned, ninety-nine-beaded necklace representing the ninety-nine names of Allah. It was said that he would bless the one reading those beads. So, for the umpteenth time that day, she began to read, "Allah is merciful, kind, compassionate." She stopped abruptly. "To whom?" she wondered. "Not to me—my mother and father beat me because I'm a girl and because they have to waste their money for my dowry. Not to me—my brothers bite and kick me for not doing their bidding quickly enough. They curse me as a woman with no brains. Does Allah only show men his kindness, mercy and compassion? Do women have no place in his care?"

At fourteen Asha had long pleaded for the privilege of attending school or even learning to read privately. Her brothers and father mocked her, "Imagine thinking that a girl could learn. She has no intelligence like a man." Even her mother had rebuked her saying, "If you learn to read and write, you will only become immoral by writing notes to strange boys!" So at the marriage ceremony, her thumb would be inked on a pad and pressed on to the paper indicating her consent.

"Is Allah so far away that he is unconcerned, not only with the daily wants and desires of a woman, but also even with her vital needs? Where will I go when I'm not able to return to my parents' home? I became a Muslim when the *molavi* whispered the *kallam* in my ears at birth, and I will die a Muslim when he whispers those words again in my ears at death; but is there nothing in between for me at all? Has Allah no concern for me as a woman? He winks at the sins of men and holds me responsible for their sins, claiming that I give off some mysterious power which leads them into immorality. Am I to blame that men are led astray?" Asha marveled at the wickedness and power she was taught that she possessed to lead men astray.

"Is Allah's justice whimsical, according to his moods, desires or needs? Are his laws flexible so that they can be bent, influenced or erased by my good works—praying, fasting, going on the pilgrimage, giving alms and reciting the creed? Do I control Allah or does he control me?" Asha worried. Her mind was in a whirl. "Is there a standard? A limit to the good I need to do? What is the maximum and how little can I get away with doing? Who sets the limits? When is this limit determined? How much do I need to be sure of paradise? Can anyone know?" her thoughts buzzed around in her head like angry bees, long suppressed and now aroused by fear for the future. "Will I ever know if I've done enough to secure a seat in paradise? What is paradise for a woman anyway?" she questioned out loud.

The ten days of *maydee* came to a close and the elders among the women arrived to bathe Asha. They poured yellow water from soaking marigolds over her body, turning her skin slightly bronze in color. Both the mother-in-law and her own mother washed their hands in the bath water, making mud casts of their hands which they placed over the door through which the groom will come. Perfume from the flowers mingled with the smoke from the wood fire. Her sisters drew intricate henna designs of good luck on the soles of her feet and over her hands. Asha rested quietly, finally submissive to the dry mud caked on both hands and feet. Her thoughts turned to her destiny. What fate has Allah written on her forehead? What is her *kismet*—her fortune or future determined by Allah and the man into whose control her life now passes?

Millions of Muslim women like Asha sit in self-inflicted mental blankness and emotional isolation, mechanically performing their required duties to survive. Millions more attempt to conceal their pondering and hurt under a light veneer of education. Still others drown their fears, doubts, and hopelessness with jewels, silks and cash.

The love of God in Christ Jesus, his Son and our Savior is the answer they need. But women controlled by his love are required to meet these needs in Muslim women's lives. Are you ready?

Sharifa Waits in the Darkness

"*Aeee-Aeee-Allah Ram Kar*" Oh, Allah be merciful! Sharifa's mother thrashed around endlessly on the woven palm mat. Women had been gathering all day to assist or observe the old toothless midwife. Sharifa stood silently watching until the midwife braced her feet against the wall and with her hands firmly on the distended abdomen attempted to correct the fetal position. Her mother's shrill scream electrified Sharifa and she raced toward the old woman, little fists flying, as she tried to free her mother from those rough hands. That action resulted in her eviction from the room.

Now Sharifa sat pondering the agony she had watched. Fingering her prayer beads, she silently recited the beautiful names of Allah. "Maybe this will help," she thought out loud. She crouched in the dark, sheltered from the wind by the family cow who placidly munched grass from the mud manger.

Many times her mother had shared the details of Sharifa's birth. Since she was their firstborn, all had vehemently desired a son. But she was only a girl!

Her father stormed from the yard and didn't return for weeks, loudly announcing his intent to divorce and find a worthy woman. Guns had been loaded and ready to fire at the good news of a son's birth. Now the bullets were removed and carefully stored. Who would waste them for the birth of a girl? No one in this family would dare to do that. What sin had this woman committed to bring such a curse on her husband?

But as time wore on, the father returned to his wife. Other children were born and died. Only their firstborn, a girl, lived. "A girl is a curse! Why have you not given me a son?" her father often screamed in the many household quarrels, "What is wrong with you, woman?" When asked how many children they had, both parents always replied, "None!" because a daughter didn't count.

Though she was only a child, Sharifa had helped in the care and burial of her siblings. She desperately joined her mother in visits to the graves of saints, pleading alongside her for a male child. Beatings, blame and curses from the father had firmly bonded mother and daughter. But she questioned, "Why do we pray to holy men rather than to Allah? Does he not hear and answer the heart cries of poor women in such need?"

"Why did Allah create women with no value except to bear sons? Why did Allah bother himself at all in creating such worthless ones?" Sharifa wondered. Treatments and new medicines devoured the little extra cash her family had, and yet no male child was born. Now this was the tenth pregnancy. "Oh, Allah, be kind and merciful to my mother. Spare her life and grant a living son to her," pleaded Sharifa.

Now alone in the darkness, Sharifa heard the high-pitched death wails of the women begin. She watched in anguish as buckets of water were carried to the room for the bathing of her mother's dead body. New clothes and a new cotton sheet were quickly readied. Suddenly, the first call for the morning prayer burst forth from the loudspeaker of the village mosque. After prayers came the announcement: "The wife of Mohammed Assalom has died and the burial will be at 10 a.m."

"Not even in death was my mother acknowledged as a person of importance," sobbed the broken-hearted little girl. "Not even in death is the name of my mother used. She is not counted worthy of even that."

No one sought her. No one brought her to view her mother for the last time before the sheet was fixed over her face. The only person who ever spoke in kindness and love to her was now silent. Only her mother had ever cared about her in any way.

Will you care about little girls lost in the darkness of Islam? Of no value in the eyes of Islam because of their gender, in the eyes of their world they are "throw-away little girls." However, in Jesus' eyes they are precious little ones for whom he died. Through which eyes do you see them?

Barvan Waits for Jezarel—the Death Angel

Lying semiconscious in the darkness, under her heavy *rozi* (a cotton-filled quilt), Barvan's emaciated skin and wizened, old body was hardly a visible presence. Age and months of illness had taken their toll on the once sturdy farm woman.

"Recite a *sura* or two from the Koran," urged her niece.

"*Ammah, say the Kallam*, the creed of Islam. You must be ready to give an answer to the Death Angel when he comes. Recite! Recite!" coaxed her grand-daughter. Mumbling was accepted as the proper response and all near her bed returned to their own conversations. The room was nearly filled and the noise was great. But Barvan had already withdrawn from ordinary events.

"Ammah, here is Mohammed Dos! You asked for him to come last week to say goodbye, but he was busy. He has come to seek your forgiveness for the harsh words with which he responded when you scolded him for stealing the landlord's jeep," the youth's father explained as he raised Barvan's bony hand to place on the young man's bowed head.

"Please, Ammah, do not die without forgiving him," pleaded the earnest father. No matter that the young man spoke not a word and his demeanor gave no indication of remorse. There had been a steady stream of relatives coming with hands folded in repentance, begging for her forgiveness. In moments of consciousness, she mused at her newly acquired power to forgive sins. Never before was this request made of her.

"Ammah, here are your prayer beads! Read them once more," pleaded her favorite nephew Isaac as he attempted to wrap the beads around her arthritic, stiff fingers. "Read, Ammah, read. Perhaps even now it will help you."

Through the gloomy haze of the crowded and stuffy room, Barvan's mind suddenly cleared and she smiled at their newfound concern for her eternal welfare. She had tried to guide these young lives into Islamic light. "Where is that light now?" she questioned. "Is this it? Offering repentance to unrepentant petitioners? Recite the Kallam? Recite the Koran? Give the right answer to the Death Angel?"

"Maybe it will help," someone said. *Maybe?*

"Is this all I have lived for?" Barvan wondered. "Will I ever be with these friends and relatives again? Is there a future?"

"My heart is filled with doubt that my good will be sufficient to outweigh my sins. My mind is in a turmoil because of the evil I have done. What happens when I die? Where do I go? What if my family doesn't recite enough suras—do I suffer even longer in hell? I do fear hell. What about paradise? I've heard that only a few women are admitted regardless of their good deeds. Will I be among the fortunate ones?"

Fear, doubt, uncertainty, and the coming judgment held her mind only briefly before she lapsed into unconsciousness again.

When next she roused, she heard the hushed voices of the men. "I've brought some opium powder. It would be easy to sprinkle the powder into her mouth and offer teaspoons of water afterward. Clearly she is dying. This would allow her to die more quickly and quietly," explained her oldest son, Khan Dos.

"I have brought ground glass. But she is no longer able to eat bread. She needs to be able to swallow it with the bread. Your way is better," responded Rafiq, her youngest son.

Unconsciousness crowded in again and there was no further clearing of her mind. Soon her breathing stopped. The ceremonial bathing of her body by the women began. Thumbs of each hand were tied securely. Great toes were tied together to be sure that she would walk a straight path. Her jaw secured with a bandage, jasmine flowers were placed in her ear lobes and around her neck. Her clothes were her very best and the white wrapping sheet was new. Neighbors and relatives gathered to cry and tear their hair from their heads by the handful. Some even beat their heads against the mud wall. Then the men came and raised the braided-rope bed to their shoulders and carried her body to the grave site where the Muslim priest led in prayers for the dead.

Peace eludes a dying Muslim. Secure hope of heaven is not a Muslim teaching. Certainty of sins forgiven is not a reality for them. Reunion with loved ones is an unknown concept.

Islamic teaching includes teaching on hell, heaven and judgment. But how a just, holy, loving God has made a certain way and offered a perfect sacrifice for our sins is unknown to Muslims.

Who will teach them?

Ilaim has worked among Muslim women for thirty-eight years as a nurse, Bible teacher, and church planter. She has worked with the Siraiki people, mainly those in the largely agricultural middle- and lower-economic class. She has traveled to various Muslim countries for the past ten years in an advisory role.

Jesus' Victory in Spiritual Warfare: "Far As The Curse Is Found!"

by Julia Colgate

I'd like to tell you a wonderful story that began before the creation of the world (Eph 1:4,5). At some moment of eternity it entered the mind of the King of Light to create a baby girl whom we will call "Beloved."

Like all things that are made, Beloved was created by Christ and for Christ (Col 1:16). She is among those called to belong to Jesus Christ (Rom 1:6), called to belong like one deeply rooted. We can hear God's call to this belonging in Ephesians 3:14-19:

> For this reason I kneel before the Father, from whom his whole family in heaven and on earth derives its name. I pray that out of his glorious riches he may strengthen you with power through his Spirit in your inner being, so that Christ may dwell in your hearts through faith. And I pray that you, being rooted and established in love, may have power, together with all the saints, to grasp how wide and long and high and deep is the love of Christ, and to know this love that surpasses knowledge-that you may be filled to the measure of the fullness of God.

We start here, because to be rooted in the love of God is Beloved's destiny.

In the Major Prophets we glimpse what was likely in God's heart as he set his affection toward Beloved. "I have loved you with an everlasting love; I have drawn you with loving-kindness" (Jer 31:3); "Before I formed you in the womb, I knew you" (Jer 1:5); "I have chosen you and have not rejected you" (Isa 41:9).

And perhaps he added, "Precious girl, you will be born into a world where there is much darkness, and you will feel like a lost child, for indeed you are vulnerable. You will feel thorns and thistles under your feet—hardships, trials, physical toil and pain. These thorns will invade your heart as well, in the form of lies which blind you so that you cannot see my perfect goodness. But do not fear! I will come soon and rescue you into my kingdom of light. Someday, Beloved, you will recognize who I really am. Someday you will realize that my passion for you is relentless, and I cannot stand to have anything separate you from me, because we belong together." And so the Lord of Beloved's origins lovingly arranged for her beginnings.

God chose the year 1957; he chose her country and her people group; he chose the religious and cultural context of folk Islam. From heaven, his eyes focused upon a quaint hillside at the northern edge of a densely populated city. He delighted to see hundreds of smiling, almond-eyed children there, skipping to school together with fingers intertwined. He saw that families there rarely moved away; this was a place to set down roots. He overheard people say, "Who would ever want to leave this fertile ground where we thrust a stick into the dirt and it grows." Indeed, the soil was rich and yielded bright green far as the eye could see.

"That's the place for my beloved," God smiled. And from that context, he carefully chose the man and the woman who would be Beloved's parents. In time, Beloved was conceived, and God was pleased. He knit her together in her mother's womb (Ps. 139:13), and he sustained her there. All the days ordained for her were written in his book before a single one had come to pass (Ps. 139:16). Then he brought Beloved out of the womb; he made her to trust in him even at her mother's breast (Ps. 22:9). Beloved was born the fourth child and would be reared in a large extended family living under one roof. These were her beginnings sovereignly chosen by God.

As always, God's intent was to root and establish Beloved in his love. But a shadow entered at this point. An enemy contested with God to bind Beloved's heart to himself. This evil one would work systematically to block her pathway from God's intent for her life. It would happen in a most natural way, cloaked in human culture.

Even before she was born, many things happened to Beloved. Beloved's family enlisted the services of the local midwife practitioner. She gave more than prenatal examinations. She had magical power to secure spiritual protection for Beloved's mother during the vulnerable times of pregnancy and childbirth. Incantations, mantras from the Koran, burning of incense and petitions to the deceased—these and other special ceremonies were enacted at certain favorable or auspicious times.

When Beloved was about one hundred days old in the womb, the midwife visited and whispered secret words over her mother's belly to help establish Beloved's destiny regarding birth, life accomplishments, marriage partner and death. At birth, Beloved's placenta was wrapped and ritualistically buried. Beloved's "twin" must be honored because, after all, the spirit of the placenta would watch over Beloved during her lifetime and accompany her at the Day of Judgment. Meanwhile Beloved was wrapped round and round in cloth and laid in bed with many "protectors" about her: red chilies hung over her bed, and a pair of tiny scissors, a clove of garlic, and her drying umbilical stump stored in a little bag near her downy head. For forty days, she would be in grave danger of attack from evil spirits attracted by blood.

On the fortieth day, a feast was held to ensure a safe passage for Beloved into childhood. The air was filled with melodic chanting in Arabic and with the smoke of incense rising from bowls. Beloved was purified of her uncleanness through circumcision. The ritualistic cleansing continued as elders of the community took scissors from a bowl of flower petals and holy water and snipped off little bits of her newborn hair. The hair trimmings would be buried in the ground. Everyone celebrated as Beloved's feet were allowed to touch the earth for the first time.

In the first weeks of Beloved's life, trusted elders performed a pilgrimage to the mountains. There at the grave site of a Muslim saint they purchased a protective charm for Beloved. Once home again, the bracelet and necklace made of knotted string were tied to Beloved's tiny body to ward off evil spirits. Beloved would not remember that these power rituals were done to her, but her life was affected nonetheless.

God watched as Beloved grew into a little child, innocently enjoying the harvest time festivities, honoring the earth goddess. She celebrated with everyone else when little children were circumcised and drops of blood fell to the ground to be united with the spirits of the earth. These rituals were enjoyed without consciousness of any negative spiritual impact. It seemed simply to be Beloved's inheritance within her folk Islamic culture. Like her parents and the generations before them, Beloved would be bound not only economically to the fertile farming fields but also religiously to the dirt of the earth itself.

Of course, Beloved had little idea of the meanings inherent in these folk traditions. Perhaps these meanings were overshadowed by an even weightier part of her identity. As she grew older, with every major Muslim holy day she would don her prayer garment and bend low in the sea of white with hundreds of her Muslim sisters. This corporate Islamic identity was an anchor for her. When local family relations were shaken by trivialities, Islam was strong. It was a larger tie that bound diverse peoples in unity all around the world. She was proud to be a Muslim—though in practice she was not devout.

Beloved learned identity from the norms of her culture. It felt good to carry out the customs of her people because each experience reinforced her belief that she was rooted in the ancient traditions of a great people. Besides, to the children, every ceremony was fun. There was good food and a chance to gather with almost everyone they knew. There was the sharing of precious grains of rice, signifying communion between neighbors and communion between humans and the spirits that sustained the rice harvest.

Did Beloved notice that her parents did not approach these ceremonies with the same light-hearted festivity as the children did? In reality, quiet desperation flowed within their hearts. They feared they might not fulfill the conditions for a safe passing from one season of life to the next. Despite this fear, however, Beloved's people to this day attest, "We could never be separated from our customs. They are our very life! They are the threads of our being! They are the strands that hold our roots in the ground."

How could they be so sure? This is how: the prince of darkness had offered Beloved's people a strange consolation for the pain of their separation from God. It was ingenious! It had just enough resemblance to truth to be a powerful counterfeit.

Satan took a number of the sharpest thorns of the cursed ground and wove a garland for Beloved to wear. She was old enough to be wooed into a clever deception. He swept her into a comprehensive system of cyclical rites to meet her needs. There was one rite for each of sixteen transitional times in life, each promising safe passage.

Satan saw that there were times when Beloved and her people felt particularly vulnerable, so he added other kinds of rites. Beloved's family sacrificed a goat in the exact center of where a foundation was laid for their new home. Later, Koranic verses were hung above the inside doorway. The family felt safe.

While these rites lent a feeling of security, they could never completely stem the tide of fear or heal the soul separated from God. And so Beloved grew up feeling uncomfortable. She and her family were experiencing the plight of all whose hearts turn away from the Lord to worship other gods. Their predicament and emotions are mirrored in Deuteronomy 28: "day after day you will be oppressed and robbed, with no one to rescue you" (verse 29); you will have "an anxious mind, eyes weary with longing, and a despairing heart. [You will live in] constant suspense, filled with dread both night and day, never sure of your life" (verses 65b,66).

When Beloved was old enough to begin to feel her own hopelessness, she chose to participate in whatever activities promised a balm for her pain. She was snagged.

If only Beloved had known how loved she really was. Instead, many disappointments tempted her not to think often of God. "What's the use of praying, when God won't give me what I need?" Beloved only knew she must protect her own wounded heart. So she trained herself not to expect anything from God, just as she did not expect anything from her earthly father who had abandoned the family to take another wife. Beloved's strategy to avoid further rejection made her appear compliant on the outside, but deep inside pride and pain isolated her from her family.

Beloved was becoming isolated from her girlfriends as well. How could this be? She had been born into the richness of a community of women who do almost everything together, often sitting close or walking arm in arm to the market. To the casual observer, there was the appearance of intimacy everywhere. But was it really so? Beloved was learning that even close friendship was not always safe for her wounded heart. Betrayals sent her most intimate friendships from the pinnacle of trust to the deep chasms of bitterness.

The fear of rejection itself made Beloved feel desperate. She tended to rebel. She was also tempted continually to manipulate people and circumstances to her advantage. "If no one will help me, then I will help myself," she vowed. She was not very successful at independence. She experienced frequent financial crises and then suffered because of vicious gossip in her community.

Sometimes her girl cousin would say to her, "Come with me to the soothsayer and we will work some magic to turn your fortune around." Usually she would reply, "What's the use? It costs too much to use magic and the effects aren't lasting." Actually, Beloved had her own ways to manipulate reality to gain what she desired. Once a victim of gossip, now she learned to wield words herself to gain power over others. When a lie was convenient, she used it to her advantage. But when the truth of her insecurity could no longer be suppressed, she hid in her bedroom and soothed herself with needlework.

When she was eighteen, Beloved was betrothed to marry. The services of the local wedding coordinator were engaged. This woman did not just plan for clothing, catering and decor. She had magical powers like the midwife had, and her role actually was to bring Beloved safely through a rite of passage.

On several occasions preceding the wedding, Beloved's body was treated with special oils. Mumbling mantras in Arabic, the wedding practitioner wafted fragrant incense over Beloved's skin. Part of Beloved's purification involved confessing all her secret sins to this practitioner. In response, the practitioner offered advice so that Beloved might achieve closure in any troubled relationships before beginning a new life with a husband.

On the night before the wedding, in an intimate ceremony, Beloved asked forgiveness for the sins of her youth to her mother and father and grandparents. Then all her elders prayed blessings over her. They whispered secret advice as they poured dippers of holy water over her head.

Beloved started her married life as one reconciled to her own family. Unfortunately, her personal preparation could not guarantee her husband's faithfulness. Shortly after their baby daughter was born, Beloved's husband began to have affairs with other women. One, two, three women—soon it was seven, eight. Beloved was devastated and enraged. Fresh rejection opened old wounds in her heart. Once again she felt as though she did not belong with the many people she had loved, including her father; and worst was the unsettled feeling she had toward God. Why was he so distant at a time like this?

After her divorce, Beloved was desperate to be free from the memory of her husband, but her intense hatred of him only created an obsession. Another man's interest in marrying her assuaged her pain. She felt cared for, until he also abandoned her. Then Beloved was convinced, "I am a reject. I belong to no one!"

The enemy of her soul sneered, "Miserable girl, you do not realize that you belong already! Every lie from your mouth is evidence that I am your true father. You belong to me. Every ritual reinstates the bond between us. Every pain reminds you that you are rejected. I will continue to use your wounds to remind you that you do not belong. Cursed were you when you were born, and now you're in even deeper—far too deep to be rescued. You might as well cooperate with me, since I'm your only hope. Here, take this coping tool called hatred. You have a right to take vengeance. This hatred should get you through the present crisis, and when you need another tool, I have plenty more."

But no coping tool, no power activity—not even the strong corporate Muslim identity—could console her heart. She felt disillusioned and shaken. Nothing seemed to matter while her deepest need was unmet.

Meanwhile, God had never taken his eye off her. He had never forgotten his intent to root and establish her in his love. And so, when the time was right, he sent her a dream to woo her heart.

Two white-robed angels visited with a special message. One placed a hand on her shoulder saying, "Realize, Beloved, that you must give yourself completely to God!"

When she woke from her dream, she hid the message in her heart and told no one. Months later she would confide to me that this dream marked the beginning of her seeking God. In the meantime, she was confused. "How can I give myself completely to God in this wretched condition? I am unacceptable. I don't belong with God. I guess I'll have to prepare myself for him first." Just the thought of having to cleanse herself from sin and overcome her own enemies was so stressful that migraine headaches came all the more frequently.

It was at this point I began to get to know Beloved. She and I had been introduced through a mutual friend. This woman's family had ministered love and shown Beloved the values of the kingdom of God. Soon I became very familiar with Beloved's migraines and toothaches, her debts and fears. Details of her personal life as a Muslim woman greatly enhanced the ethnographic study I had been conducting. I found Beloved intriguing and winsome. But I was troubled by her continual struggle. Her pain triggered something in me that made me feel awkward and helpless. And so, by the time I had concluded that this girl was a total mess, I had also set myself up to remain fairly detached. Eventually I felt deeply convicted that while I stood by watching, this special new friend was only falling deeper into the darkness. I decided it was time to invest my heart. I loved Beloved enough now to understand her captivity.

One afternoon, she visited me at my home. Her facial expression told it all: she was suffering another migraine headache. She confessed to me, "Something is weighing heavily upon me. If I tell you about it, maybe the burden will lift. Would you mind, could we talk?"

"Sure," I said, "but there is something I need to do first. You go home and I'll come to you later." I asked for time because I needed to pray. I needed more than world-view insight today. I needed love; and I needed the power of the Holy Spirit. So I bowed on my prayer rug. And the Lord did something that would change forever the way I see people like Beloved and the way I see myself.

God drew me into worship very quickly. As I adored him, I became acutely aware of my unworthiness. In fact, I felt ashamed. I felt reduced to absolute neediness. Suddenly I sensed I was standing before the cross of Christ. I resisted the temptation to turn and run. Instead I lingered and gazed upon Jesus in his sufferings. I began to cry. "Lord Jesus, I am sick. I am dirty. I am empty. I am as tempted and ensnared as any woman can be. I am unacceptable. I hate to see you suffer like this, but Jesus, I need you to suffer for me. Please help me. Please heal me."

Then I remembered Beloved. In my spirit I eagerly brought her to my side before the cross. There I wept with compassion. For God had caused me suddenly to be able to identify with all of Beloved's sins and sorrows. I repented. Here, all along, I had been keeping my distance. But God wanted me to see that under all the practices unique to our different cultures, our hearts are much the same. I am like Beloved. I am like this folk Muslim woman. So now, here we stood—two women feeling unworthy and far from home. And by his sufferings Jesus communicated, "You are unworthy, but you are worth everything to me!"

Then God did something only he could do. He swept me into bold intercession for Beloved, for her salvation and for her healing. Imagine how stunned I felt as it dawned on me that my sameness with Beloved was somehow the condition for my helping to set her free!

Deep in prayer, I saw Beloved smiling nervously and waving her arms before me as if to shield me from seeing something. In my spirit, I sensed it meant she was keeping a secret from me. Then I saw a clear picture of an old Asian man balding with long hair. I did not know who he was. But the Lord impressed me that Beloved was in trouble and it had to do with an unholy tie to this man. I felt urged by the Lord to visit Beloved at her house. When I rose from prayer I was excited about what the Lord would do. Could this be the night of Beloved's salvation?

I found her with her family gathered around the television in their small living room. So that I could talk alone with Beloved, I asked her if she might be willing to give me a haircut before I left town the next day. She led me into the small room that is her neighborhood beauty salon. I let my eyes peruse the walls. In the mirror, I noticed behind me a portrait of her ex-husband (whom she despises) displayed prominently above the doorframe for the sake of their daughter. Then my eyes fell on another picture close by, and guess whom I saw? It was the old man whose image the Lord had shown me earlier when I was praying.

"Who is that old man in the picture?" I asked her quietly.

"He is my ex-husband's grandfather. He is a powerful sorcerer." I caught my breath as I recognized my cue from the Lord. I was to take a step of faith.

"Beloved, you know I love you. You know I pray for you. When I was in prayer for you this afternoon, God showed me that man's face. Then I sensed that you are in some kind of bondage from which God wants to free you. That is why I am here now. Is there something you want to tell me?"

She smiled broadly and relaxed as she realized that God had broken into her secrets. She hesitated and then slowly began her story. "Actually I have kept two secrets from you. The first is that for several years my ex-husband has been pursuing me. He cries, 'Take me back!' And I answer, 'I'll never take you back, even if you cry tears of blood!' Before now I have not told you that I think my migraine headaches are partly related to my hatred of this man.

"But there is more. I have never told you this, but every Thursday evening after the last call to prayer, I experience a terrible itch that covers my whole body. It torments me until the first call to prayer the next morning. I spend the whole night in misery and when I rise in the morning there is no rash, no scratch marks. This has happened to me every Thursday night for the last three years!" (Thursday night is a "power time" for folk Muslims.) It was apparent to both of us that Beloved was under a curse. Beloved was aware that the curse had come from the old man at the request of her embittered ex-husband.

I saw Beloved straighten with purpose. She suddenly wished to burn the two portraits from her walls. "Wait!" I said. "Don't do it in hatred. If you do, you'll have given the enemy another victory. You must bless your enemy and forgive, then you'll be on God's side!" We held the framed photos in our hands, and I modeled for Beloved how to speak blessing to these two enemies in Jesus' name.

I asked, "Do you know how you can become freed from the itching curse?"

She thought. Her answer showed she had been reflecting on God's call to her: "I think I must prepare to present myself to God."

I answered gently, "Beloved, it is not possible for you to make yourself acceptable to God. But God has made a way for you. You can trust in the blood of Jesus and simply cry out to God in your neediness." I offered to pray with her, but she said, "That's okay. I know just what to do!" So I went home.

The next day was the infamous Thursday, a "power time." Beloved came to me and told me simply that she had prayed and burned the portraits after our time together. Now she waited for the sun to set. Would she itch?

The following day, Beloved brought me the great news that she had not itched at all the previous night! She hoped that she had been set free from the curse in the name of Jesus the Messiah! She confessed she was aware that God was calling her to himself and that she desired to follow me in my faith in Jesus. I responded, "If what I suspect is true, Beloved, this freedom from itching is just the start of a mighty deliverance for you. There will probably be many other things we need to talk about."

Meanwhile, the Lord confirmed his mercy to Beloved. Thursday after Thursday passed, with no itching! Glory to God!

The stress in Beloved's life was still high. One day, her head was pounding, and I offered to pray for her. We knelt and raised our hands slightly in prayer and bowed. Startling me at first, Beloved repeated each phrase of my prayer for healing for her headache including thanks for the power of the shed blood of Jesus. Amen! When we lifted our heads, she looked at me wide-eyed and said, "In the middle of our prayer, my headache lifted suddenly!" We hugged, with tears in our eyes. She asked, "Why do you think the headache went away?" I answered, "Because God loves you! And he heard our prayer in Jesus' name."

I sensed that Beloved was waking to the Light. One day she said to me, "I realize I am consumed with hatred toward my ex-husband. I should forgive him."

I answered, "Yes, then you will not be imprisoned by your unforgiveness!"

Then, in a dramatic "power ritual" of her own initiative, she wrote her grievances against her ex-husband and forgave them one by one in the name of Jesus. Then she held the paper representing her hatred and said, "This is Satan to me, so now I will burn it!" And she did! The next morning her heart was at peace. She reported, "I am freed from my bondage to hatred!"

Soon her family experienced a severe trial. In the night, Beloved was sleepless and decided that she would pray on her own for help: "O God, in the name of Jesus the Messiah, by virtue of the perfect sacrifice blood that he shed, I ask you to give me peace." Suddenly a peace from heaven flooded her heart and the anxiety was totally gone!

Each time such mercy came to her, Beloved questioned the lies by which the enemy had held her captive all these years through her pain of not belonging. With every intervention of God's truth and power, and with every exposure to the love of the community of believers, Beloved would express to me, "I believe God is calling me to give my whole self to him, one hundred percent!" As I watched with joy, I realized that the root affection of her heart was loosening from the lies of the curse. She was getting ready to shift her allegiance to the One who was truly caring for all her needs. Her deepest heart was discovering, "This must be to whom I belong."

Indeed, within weeks, Jesus had so wooed Beloved's heart that she had to respond. She came one afternoon, saying, "I feel compelled to give myself to Jesus the Messiah! Something urges me to act today. God has answered my prayers for help, freed me from the itching curse, miraculously healed my headaches, calmed my anxiety, all at the name of Jesus the Messiah, by his blood!" She continued, "Whenever I cry for help in the name of Jesus, there is always a touch of peace and healing! I am willing to give myself to him now. I haven't been ready before. But now the powerful touches of God that left peace have convinced me."

We knelt and prayed. After declaring her faith, she prayed, "I ask you, Lord Jesus Christ, to rule my heart from within." Beloved was a believer now! I felt relieved that she was already in the kingdom. And yet, in the weeks that followed, I sensed that God was still in earnest pursuit of her, as if she still needed to be delivered from captivity.

"Lord, I don't understand. Is this really necessary?"

God answered, "Yes! And just wait till you see the rescue I have planned for you, my beloved!"

Months passed. One night after my husband and children were asleep, I stole out of bed and spread my prayer rug on the living room floor. I said, "Lord, I trust you to be good to me. So I will open myself wide to you. Tell me, what is this intense ache I feel inside? I invite you, Lord, to take apart the ache and tell me what it is made of."

I lay on my face on the floor and waited. I imagined him examining my deepest heart. To be candid with you, I half-expected rebuke, for I tended toward self-condemnation.

I was surprised when he said clearly, "You long to belong."

"Oh." When he put my ache into words, I felt the pain even more. I admitted, "Lord, this must be true, for my heart is breaking at your words. Even with the blessing of friends and family and all the activities of my faith, I feel lonely. I long to belong. You have seen it." I wept and wept.

I kept my heart before the Lord and allowed myself to hurt. I felt that I could relate now to anyone from any culture who has felt the pain of not belonging.

Suddenly he spoke sweetly, "There is a Julia-shaped place in my heart. That is where you belong."

I cried with joy, "O Lord, take me there! I will ache with misery until I am at rest in that place in your heart."

After I identified my pain of not belonging, God aggressively began to show me what I had done with my pain all these years. I had hidden within myself. I had claimed the right to anger. I had resigned to guilt and self-condemnation. As the Lord exposed me, I became disillusioned with all the ways I had coped. "Well, this is an unpleasant surprise! It seems the safe places I had created for myself only became strongholds of the enemy. Lord, save me!"

After the disillusionment, Jesus employed his truth and power and the love of my sisters in Christ to enact an amazing rescue from deception. The first wave of this rescue lasted several months. Mercy after mercy flowed my way. "O Lord, your love toward me is so dramatic that I feel startled! I don't have a history of occult practice like Beloved does as a folk Muslim. So why is your powerful intervention so necessary for me?"

"Because there are still many lies buried in the pain of your past. These lies hold your affections so that you cannot give your whole self to me. I am jealous for your love. So I will battle your lies one by one and set you free to be one with me.

Dear sisters, can you see that Jesus is engaged in spiritual warfare by wooing us? Spiritual warfare is Jesus' work to root us in his love by securing the affection of our whole heart. He wants us to belong. This is his desire for you and me and all the Muslim women we will ever meet.

There is a reason why God moved the Apostle Paul to write Ephesians 3:17. God knows that many of us who are already in the Kingdom are not yet rooted and established in his love. And in this regard, we are just like our Muslim friends. Perhaps like them, we have not even dared to imagine we might belong to God in this sweet and powerful way the Scriptures speak of, because there is so much rejection in us. When we are aware of our sameness with Muslim women, living among them becomes a journey together out of the curse and into the love of God.

Our wonderful Lord knows just what to do to rescue us into belonging. Let me describe to you His spiritual warfare for us. He came into our every human experience and became familiar with all our temptations, but without sin. He came to destroy the devil's work (1 Jn 3:8), so he plunged right into our darkness. He participated in human traditions and rites of passage. He so perfectly associated with us "unacceptables" that he himself was regarded as unacceptable and was rejected by men.

In the final hours, Jesus knew what it would cost to "make His blessings flow far as the curse is found." Men took a thorny vine and wove it into a mock crown (Matt 27:29). Jesus did not refuse the thorns pressed into his brow. In fact, every single thorn had meaning for Jesus. To every thorny lie that has ever deceived us, Jesus said "Let me have it." And as he faced our lies, he suffered in his soul. He tasted the most essential questions of our hearts. "Is God good? Is God just? Will he love me?" This is how deeply Jesus entered into our pain of not belonging. Hanging on the cross, Jesus felt unacceptability and rejection. We know this because in an hour of tremendous darkness, he cried out, from the lament of Psalm 22, "My God, my God, why have you forsaken me?" (Matt 27:45,46)

He suffered immensely. Having taken on the sins of the whole world, his shame was so great that it swallowed up our shame. He redeemed us from the curse by becoming accursed for us, as the Scriptures say (Gal 3:13). In this, he dealt a crushing blow to the enemy; for when he went down into death, he plunged to the very core of the curse, through all the layers of bondage and deceptions of world view, and he broke the power of the evil one (Col 2:15)!

It is written that he will see the result of the suffering of his soul and be satisfied (Isa 53:11). Sisters, it is finished! (John 19:30) Jesus says triumphantly to us today, "See, I have taken your thorns upon my brow. Every thorn is a lie that has kept you far from me. In my death, I penetrate the darkness to bring you out, because it's time to come home—you and your Muslim friends. Come home to my love and become rooted and established there. We belong together."

A Responsive Prayer to the Lord

O Lord, we hear you calling to us. We confess that we are unacceptable. We don't belong and we feel miserable. Today our hearts respond with a cry: Jesus, bring us home! Have your way with us at the depths of our affections. Set us free from the lies that bind us. Purify the aches in our hearts. Then use us to accompany Muslim women along the journey until together we all are rooted in Your love. We cry out to you now for the fulfillment of all that you have desired from eternity. For the sake of Jesus, our most Beloved—Amen.

Julia Colgate lives with her husband and children in a Muslim urban village where the community of women is very strong. She has enjoyed meaningful relationships with Muslim women since moving to the region in 1990.